First World War

and Army of Occupation

War Diary

France, Belgium and Germany

57 DIVISION
172 Infantry Brigade,
Brigade Machine Gun Company
21 October 1916 - 28 February 1918

WO95/2985/11

The Naval & Military Press Ltd
www.nmarchive.com
Published in association with The National Archives

Published by

The Naval & Military Press Ltd

Unit 10 Ridgewood Industrial Park,

Uckfield, East Sussex,

TN22 5QE England

Tel: +44 (0) 1825 749494

www.naval-military-press.com

www.nmarchive.com

This diary has been reprinted in facsimile from the original. Any imperfections are inevitably reproduced and the quality may fall short of modern type and cartographic standards.

Contents

Document type	Place/Title	Date From	Date To
Heading	WO95/2985/11 57 Divn. 172 Inf Brig Brig M/G Co. 1917 Feb-1918 Feb		
Heading	57th Division 172nd Infy Bde 172nd Machine Gun Coy Feb 1917-Feb 1918		
Heading	War Diary Of 172 Machine Gun Company From 13th February 1917 To 28th February 1917 Volume 1		
Miscellaneous	From O/c 172 Machine Gun Company		
War Diary	Grantham	21/10/1916	13/02/1917
War Diary	Southampton	14/02/1917	14/02/1917
War Diary	Havre	15/02/1917	16/02/1917
War Diary	Abbeville	17/02/1917	17/02/1917
War Diary	Bailleul	18/02/1917	18/02/1917
War Diary	Swartenbrouch	18/02/1917	23/02/1917
War Diary	Estaires	23/02/1917	24/02/1917
War Diary	Bois Grenier	25/02/1917	28/02/1917
War Diary	Bois Grenier France	01/03/1917	11/03/1917
War Diary	Bois Grenier	12/03/1917	31/03/1917
Miscellaneous	From O/c 172nd Machine Gun Company		
War Diary	Bois Grenier	01/04/1917	25/04/1917
War Diary	Rue Du Bois	26/04/1917	30/04/1917
Operation(al) Order(s)	Operation Order No. 1 By Capt. G.A. Wade Commanding 172nd Machine Gun Company	10/04/1917	10/04/1917
Map	Map		
Miscellaneous	172 Machine Gun Company	10/04/1917	10/04/1917
Operation(al) Order(s)	Operation Order No. 2 By Capt. G.A. Wade Commanding 172nd Machine Gun Coy	16/04/1917	16/04/1917
Miscellaneous	172 Machine Gun Company	01/05/1917	01/05/1917
Operation(al) Order(s)	Operation Order No. 3 By Capt. G.A. Wade Commanding 172nd Machine Gun Company	24/04/1917	24/04/1917
War Diary	Rue Du Bois and Bois Grenier Sectors	01/05/1917	31/05/1917
Heading	War Diary Of 172nd Machine Gun Company Period 1st June 1917 To 30th June 1917		
War Diary	Rue Du Bois and Bois Grenier	01/06/1917	30/06/1917
Operation(al) Order(s)	Operation Order No. 5 By Capt. G.A. Wade Commanding 172nd M.G.Coy	15/06/1917	15/06/1917
Operation(al) Order(s)	Operation Order No. 6 By Capt. G.A. Wade Commanding 172nd Machine Gun Company	25/06/1917	25/06/1917
Miscellaneous	Appendix 1		
Miscellaneous	Appendix II		
Map	Map		
Miscellaneous	From O.C. 172 M G Coy	01/08/1917	01/08/1917
War Diary	Bois Grenier And Rue Du Bois Sectors	01/07/1917	31/07/1917
Miscellaneous	From O.C. 172 Machine Gun Coy	01/09/1917	01/09/1917
War Diary	Bois Grenier and Rue Du Bois Sub Sectors	01/08/1917	31/08/1917
Operation(al) Order(s)	Operation Order No. 9	23/07/1917	23/07/1917
Heading	No.172 Machine Gun Coy War Diary September 1917		
Operation(al) Order(s)	Operation Order No. 10 By Capt. G.A. Wade Commdg 172nd M G Coy	15/09/1917	15/09/1917
Miscellaneous	Relief Table		

Miscellaneous	Certificate To Be Obtained From Each relieving Gun Team		
War Diary	Bois Grenier and Rue Du Bois	01/09/1917	16/09/1917
War Diary	Estaires	17/09/1917	24/09/1917
War Diary	Pippemont	25/09/1917	30/09/1917
War Diary	Pippemont S 15 Central	01/10/1917	04/10/1917
War Diary	Pippemont Therouanne S.15. Central	05/10/1917	17/10/1917
War Diary	Ref. Map Hazebrouck 5A Belgium 1.100,000	18/10/1917	24/10/1917
War Diary	Sheet 28 Belgium France F.8.c	25/10/1917	25/10/1917
War Diary	Ref. Maps Sheet 28 N.W. 1/20000 Sheet 19.20.27.28 1.40000	26/10/1917	28/10/1917
War Diary	Map Broembeek 1.10000	29/10/1917	31/10/1917
War Diary	Map Belgium France Sheet 28 1.40000	01/11/1917	01/11/1917
War Diary	Schaap Bailie 1.10000	02/11/1917	06/11/1917
Miscellaneous	172 Inf Bde	01/12/1917	01/12/1917
War Diary	Map Hazebrouck 5A	07/11/1917	29/11/1917
War Diary	Hazebrouck 5A 2A40.01	30/11/1917	30/11/1917
Miscellaneous	172nd Inf. Bde	01/11/1917	01/11/1917
War Diary	Berthem	01/12/1917	06/12/1917
War Diary	Herzeele	07/12/1917	16/12/1917
War Diary	Elverdinghe	17/12/1917	23/12/1917
War Diary	Signal Farm V21c.1505	24/12/1917	24/12/1917
War Diary	Houthulst Forest Sector	24/12/1917	31/12/1917
Operation(al) Order(s)	172 M.G. Coy Operation Order A	23/12/1917	23/12/1917
Operation(al) Order(s)	Operation Order B by O.C. Patter	31/12/1917	31/12/1917
Operation(al) Order(s)	Operation Order C by O.C. 172 M.G. Coy	31/12/1917	31/12/1917
War Diary	Belgium Sheet 28.N.W.	01/01/1918	03/01/1918
War Diary	Belgium & France Sheet 36	04/01/1918	12/01/1918
War Diary	Ref. Maps Houplines & Bois Grenier	13/01/1918	16/01/1918
War Diary	Ref. Maps Houplines & Bois Grenier 1.10000	17/01/1918	20/01/1918
War Diary	Ref Map Belgium & France Sheet 36	21/01/1918	26/01/1918
War Diary	Ref Maps Houplines and Bois Grenier	27/01/1918	30/01/1918
Miscellaneous	Relief Of 171st Machine Gun Coy		
Miscellaneous	Relief Order		
Miscellaneous	Relief Of 171 M.G. Coy	26/01/1918	26/01/1918
Miscellaneous		26/01/1918	26/01/1918
War Diary	Ref Maps Houplines and Bois Grenier	01/02/1918	14/02/1918
War Diary	Sheet 36A N.E.	15/02/1918	18/02/1918
War Diary	Ref Maps Sheet 36A N.E.	19/02/1918	28/02/1918
Operation(al) Order(s)	Operation Order No. 12 172nd Machine Gun Company	20/02/1918	20/02/1918
Operation(al) Order(s)	Operation Order No. 10 172nd M G Coy	31/01/1918	31/01/1918
Miscellaneous	Group Commanders Orders	30/01/1918	30/01/1918
Miscellaneous	Relief Orders	01/01/1918	01/01/1918
Miscellaneous	Relief Of 171 M.G. Coy	04/02/1918	04/02/1918
Miscellaneous	Relief Table	04/02/1918	04/02/1918
Operation(al) Order(s)	172nd Machine Gun Coy Order No. 11		
Miscellaneous	Relief Of 172 Machine Gun Company	16/02/1918	16/02/1918
Map	Map		

WO 95 2965/11

57 Dnn: 172 Inf Brig

Brig M/G Co.

1917 Feb - 1918 Feb

57TH DIVISION
172ND INFY BDE

172ND MACHINE GUN COY.

FEB 1917-FEB 1918

57.

Vol 1

Confidential

War Diary

— of —

172 Machine Gun Company.

From 13th February 1917. to 28th February 1917

Volume 1.

H/18.

From O/C 172 Machine Gun Company
To D.A.G 3rd Echelon Base

Herewith diary of above Coy
from 13.2.17 to 28.2.17
please

G.A. White Capt.
O/C 172 Machine Gun Coy

5.3.17

Instructions regarding War Diaries and Intelligence Summaries are contained in F. S. Regs., Part II. and the Staff Manual respectively. Title Pages will be prepared in manuscript.

WAR DIARY

~~or~~

~~INTELLIGENCE SUMMARY~~

(Erase heading not required.)

Army Form C. 2118.

172 Machine Gun Company

Place	Date	Hour	Summary of Events and Information	Remarks and references to Appendices
GRANTHAM	21.10.16		Company formed	
GRANTHAM	13.2.17	4.30pm	Company left BELTON PARK for GRANTHAM STATION.	
		9.25pm	Entrained GRANTHAM STATION for SOUTHAMPTON	
SOUTHAMPTON	14.2.17	6.30am	arrived and detrained	
		6.30pm	Embarked for FRANCE	
			The following Officers embarked with the Company	
			CAPT G. A. WADE. LT C. M. HOWARD. LT P. McGRATH. LT J. A. BARRACLOUGH	
			2ND LT W. G. DONALDSON. 2ND LT L. E. M. ACKROYD. 2ND LT O. GREENWOOD	
			2ND LT E. C. JONES. 2ND LT C. H. GADD. 2ND LT W. JAMES.	
HAVRE	15.2.17	2.30pm	Arrived	
		3pm	Disembarked	
		7pm	Marched to and arrived at No 5 REST CAMP	
	16.2.17	4pm	Left No 5 REST CAMP	
		9.20pm	Entrained	

C. Wade Capt
O.C. 172 M.G.C.

2449 Wt. W14957/M90 750,000 1/16 J.B.C. & A. Forms/C.2118/12.

Instructions regarding War Diaries and Intelligence Summaries are contained in F. S. Regs., Part II. and the Staff Manual respectively. Title Pages will be prepared in manuscript.

WAR DIARY

~~INTELLIGENCE SUMMARY~~

(Erase heading not required.)

172 Machine Gun Company

Army Form C. 2118.

Place	Date	Hour	Summary of Events and Information	Remarks and references to Appendices
ABBEVILLE	17.2.17	7.30 pm	Arrived	
		9.30 pm	Left ABBEVILLE	
BAILLEUL	18.2.17	8.15 am	Arrived and detrained	
SWARTENBROUCH		12 noon	Marched to and arrived at billets	
	19.2.17		Carried out Company training at SWARTENBROUCH	
	20.2.17		Carried out Company training at SWARTENBROUCH	
	21.2.17		Carried out Company training at SWARTENBROUCH	
	22.2.17		Carried out Company training at SWARTENBROUCH	
	23.2.17	10 am	Left SWARTENBROUCH	
ESTAIRES		1.15 pm	Arrived and billeted in the town	
	24.2.17	2 pm	Left ESTAIRES and arrived at Headquarters and billets of 2nd ANZAC Machine Gun Coy. H 22 b 6 4 (Ref map 36 NW 4 $\frac{1}{10,000}$) at 5 pm.	
		7 pm	Relieved 2nd ANZAC Machine Gun Coy in trenches BOIS GRENIER No 3 Section at rest. Transport billeted at H 3 c 7 3	E. W. Cruse Capt O.C. 172 MG Coy

2449 Wt. W14957/M90 750,000 1/16 J.B.C. & A. Forms/C.2118/12.

Army Form C. 2118.

Instructions regarding War Diaries and Intelligence Summaries are contained in F. S. Regs., Part II. and the Staff Manual respectively. Title Pages will be prepared in manuscript.

WAR DIARY
or
~~INTELLIGENCE SUMMARY~~
(Erase heading not required.)

172 Machine Gun Company

Place	Date	Hour	Summary of Events and Information	Remarks and references to Appendices
BOIS. GRENIER	25.2.17		Nos 1, 2 & 4 Sections in trenches	
	26.2.17		Nos 1, 2 & 4 Sections in trenches 1 O.R. killed	
	27.2.17		Nos 1, 2 & 4 Sections in trenches 1 O.R. wounded	
	28.2.17		Nos 1, 2 & 4 Sections in trenches. Indirect fire was carried on MONT PINDO and LA HOUSSOIE:	
				[signature] Capt. O.C. 172 M.G. Coy

2449 Wt. W14957/M90 750,000 1/16 J.B.C. & A. Forms/C.2118/12.

Original

Instructions regarding War Diaries and Intelligence Summaries are contained in F. S. Regs., Part II. and the Staff Manual respectively. Title Pages will be prepared in manuscript.

WAR DIARY
or
~~INTELLIGENCE SUMMARY~~

(Erase heading not required.)

Army Form C. 2118. 37

172nd Machine Gun Company

Vol 2

Place	Date	Hour	Summary of Events and Information	Remarks and references to Appendices
BOIS. GRENIER FRANCE	1.3.17		Nos 1 2 & 4 Sections in Trenches. Indirect fire carried out on HALT at MONT. PINDO I 34 a 2 4 & DISTILLERY at LA HOUSSOIE I 27 b 5 5 (By Map 36 N.W.4 1/10000)	
	2.3.17		Nos 1 2 & 4 Sections in Trenches. Indirect fire carried out as above.	
	3.3.17		No 3 Section relieved No 4 Section at 2pm. Indirect fire carried out on LE BAS HAU O 2 d 1 7 and Fme HOUSSAIN O 2 a 3 7.	
	4.3.17		Nos 1 2 & 3 Sections in Trenches. Indirect fire carried out as on 3.3.17	
	5.3.17		Nos 1 2 & 3 Sections in Trenches	
	6.3.17		Nos 1 2 & 3 Sections in Trenches. Indirect fire carried out on GRANDE. MAISNIL Fme I 33 d 0 3 and HOUSSAIN Fme O 2 a 3 7	
	7.3.17		Nos 1 2 & 3 Sections in Trenches	
	8.3.17		Nos 1 2 & 3 Sections in Trenches. Indirect fire carried out on LE. BAS. HAU and Fme HOUSSAIN	
	9.3.17		No 4 Section relieved No 1 Section at 2pm. Indirect fire carried out as on 8.3.17	
	10.3.17		Nos 2 3 & 4 Sections in trenches. Indirect fire carried out on FARM O 2 c 7 4 and DISTILLERY I 27 b 5 5	
	11.3.17		Nos 2. 3 & 4 Sections in Trenches. Indirect fire carried out on DISTILLERY and Road near BATTERY. HQ 36 O 2 c 3 3	

C. A. Wade Capt.
O.C. 172 M.G. Coy

2449 Wt. W14957/M90 750,000 1/16 J.B.C. & A. Forms/C.2118/12.

WAR DIARY
or
~~INTELLIGENCE SUMMARY~~
(Erase heading not required.)

Army Form C. 2118.

Instructions regarding War Diaries and Intelligence Summaries are contained in F. S. Regs., Part II. and the Staff Manual respectively. Title Pages will be prepared in manuscript.

172nd Machine Gun Company

Place	Date	Hour	Summary of Events and Information	Remarks and references to Appendices
BOIS GRENIER	12.3.17		No 2 3 + 4 Sections in Trenches. Indirect fire carried out on Farm at O2c74	
	13.3.17		No 2 3 + 4 Sections in Trenches. Indirect fire carried out as above	
	14.3.17		No 2 3 + 4 Sections in Trenches. Indirect fire carried out on ROAD near BATTERY HOUSE	
	15.3.17		No 2 3 + 4 Sections in Trenches. Indirect fire carried out on THE GAP O2b41 and THE HOTEL at LA HOUSSOIE I27c89	
	16.3.17		No 1 Section relieved No 2 Section at 2 pm. Indirect fire carried out on BACQUART O7a96 and the road near BATTERY HOUSE. Lt J. A. BARRACLOUGH attached to 170 Machine Gun Coy	
	17.3.17		No 1 3 + 4 Sections in the Trenches. Indirect fire carried out on LE QUESNE I33a69 and HALT MONT. PINDO	
	18.3.17		No 1 3 + 4 Sections in the Trenches.	
	19.3.17		No 1 3 + 4 Sections in the Trenches.	
	20.3.17		No 1 3 + 4 Sections in the Trenches. Indirect fire carried out on BAS MAISNIL and GRANDE MARAIS.	
	21.3.17		No 1 3 + 4 Sections in the Trenches. Indirect fire carried out as on 20.3.17. Lt J. A. BARRACLOUGH transferred to 170 Machine Gun Company as 2nd IN COMMAND	
	22.3.17		No 1 3 + 4 Sections in the Trenches. Indirect fire carried out as on 20.3.17	
	22.3.17		No 2 Section relieved No 3 Section. 2/Lieut M. C. VYVYAN reported and taken on strength of Coy	[signature] Capt. O.C. 172 M.G. Coy

2449 Wt. W14957/M90 750,000 1/16 J.B.C. & A. Forms/C.2118/12.

Army Form C. 2118.

Instructions regarding War Diaries and Intelligence Summaries are contained in F. S. Regs., Part II. and the Staff Manual respectively. Title Pages will be prepared in manuscript.

WAR DIARY

~~or INTELLIGENCE SUMMARY~~ 172nd Machine Gun Company

(Erase heading not required.)

Place	Date	Hour	Summary of Events and Information	Remarks and references to Appendices
BOIS GRENIER	24.3.17		No 1 2 & 4 Sections in the Trenches. Indirect fire carried out on LE BAS HAU and Road near BATTERY HQ in conjunction with 171 Machine Gun Company on our Right.	
	25.3.17		No 1.2 & 4 Sections in the Trenches.	
	26.3.17		No 1.2 & 4 Sections in the Trenches.	
	27.3.17		No 1 2 & 4 Section in the Trenches	
	28.3.17		No 1 2 & 4 Sections in the Trenches. 171st Brigade relieved 172nd Brigade	
	29.3.17		No 1 2 & 4 Sections in the Trenches	
	30.3.17		No 3 Section relieved No 4 Section.	
	31.3.17		No 1.2 & 3 Sections in the Trenches	

E. A. [illegible] Capt
O.C. 172 M.G. Coy.

2449 Wt. W14957/M90 750,000 1/16 J.B.C. & A. Forms/C.2118/12.

H/298

From O/C 172nd Machine Gun Company
To D A G 3rd Echelon Base

Herewith original Diary of above Company for April 1917 please

[signature] Capt
O.C. 172 Machine Gun Coy.

Original

Instructions regarding War Diaries and Intelligence Summaries are contained in F. S. Regs., Part II. and the Staff Manual respectively. Title Pages will be prepared in manuscript.

WAR DIARY ~~or~~ INTELLIGENCE SUMMARY

(Erase heading not required.)

Army Form C. 2118.

172 Machine Gun Company 37/57

Vol 3

Place	Date	Hour	Summary of Events and Information	Remarks and references to Appendices
BOIS GRENIER	1.4.17		No 1 2 & 3 Sections in the trenches. Strength of company on this date 199 - 10 officers 180 ORs and 7 attached Signallers	
	2.4.17		No 1 2 & 3 Sections in the trenches	
	3.4.17		No 1 2 & 3 Sections in the trenches	
	4.4.17		No 1 2 & 3 Sections in the trenches	
	5.4.17		No 1 2 & 3 Section in the trenches. Indirect fire carried out on DISTILLERY ROAD I 27 b 8 5. RATION DUMP at I 27 c 1 1 and THE BREWERY I 22 c 9 4 Map ref BOIS GRENIER $\frac{1}{10000}$ 36 N W 4	
	6.4.17		No 4 Section relieved No 1 Section. Indirect fire carried out on ROAD JUNCTION N 12 a 1 2 CHATEAU RICHE N 11 D and BOIS BLANCS I 32 b. Map ref. RADINGHEM $\frac{1}{10000}$ 36 S W 2	
	7.4.17		No 2 3 & 4 Sections in the trenches. Indirect fire carried out on Road FARM HOUSSAIN O 2 a HOUSE and ROAD N 11 a 8 3 (Ref map RADINGHEM $\frac{1}{10000}$ 36 S W 2) and Road I 33 d 1 5 map ref BOIS GRENIER $\frac{1}{10000}$ 36 N W 4	
	8.4.17		No 2 3 & 4 in the trenches	
	9.4.17		No 2 3 & 4 in the trenches	

2449 Wt. W14957/M90 750,000 1/16 J.B.C. & A. Forms/C.2118/12.

Instructions regarding War Diaries and Intelligence Summaries are contained in F. S. Regs., Part II. and the Staff Manual respectively. Title Pages will be prepared in manuscript.

WAR DIARY ~~or~~ INTELLIGENCE SUMMARY

(Erase heading not required.)

Army Form C. 2118.

172 Machine Gun Company

Place	Date	Hour	Summary of Events and Information	Remarks and references to Appendices
BOIS GRENIER	10.4.17		Nos 2 3 & 4 Sections in the trenches. 10 guns co-operated with the Artillery and Trench Mortars in forming a box barrage	See appendix I
BOIS GRENIER	11.4.17		Nos 2 3 & 4 Sections in the Trenches. 2/Lt W JAMES admitted to Hospital. He accidentally knelt on a condenser bag whilst the gun was in action on the night of the 10th instant and scalded his knee	
	12.4.17		Nos 2 3 & 4 Sections in the trenches	
	13.4.17		No 1 Section relieved No 2 Section	
	14.4.17		Nos 1 3 & 4 Sections in the Trenches. Indirect fire carried out on BAS MAISNIL N 12 a (map ref RADINGHEM 1/10000 36 S W 2) HALT at MONT PINDO I 34 a (map ref BOIS GRENIER 1/10000 36 N W 4) FARM at O 2 c 7 4. BACQUART O 7 a ROAD JUNCTION N 12 b 50 15 CHATEAU RICHE N 11 d (map ref RADINGHEM 1/10000 36 S W 2)	
	15.4.17		Nos 1 3 & 4 Sections in the trenches	
	16.4.17		Nos 1 3 & 4 Sections in the Trenches 10 guns co-operated with the artillery and Trench Mortars in forming a box barrage	See appendix II

Instructions regarding War Diaries and Intelligence Summaries are contained in F. S. Regs., Part II. and the Staff Manual respectively. Title Pages will be prepared in manuscript.

WAR DIARY
or
INTELLIGENCE SUMMARY

(Erase heading not required.)

Army Form C. 2118.

172 Machine Gun Company.

Place	Date	Hour	Summary of Events and Information	Remarks and references to Appendices
BOIS GRENIER	16.4.17		Continued. The guns of No 4 Section carried out Indirect fire on GRANDE MAISNIL FARM I 33 c and d. (Map ref BOIS GRENIER 1/10000 36 N W 4) FARM O 2 c 7 4 and ROAD near BATTERY HOUSE O 2 c (Map ref RADINGHEM 1/10000 36 S W 2)	
	17.4.17		No 1.3 & 4 Sections in Trenches. Indirect fire carried out on DISTILLERY. LA HOUSSOIE LE QUESNE. BREWERY I 22 c. ROAD I 33 d 1.3. LE BAS HAU CROSS ROADS WEZ MACQUART. FARM O 2 c 7 4.	
	18.4.17		No 1 3 & 4 Sections in the Trenches. Indirect fire carried out on Road near BATTERY HOUSE, THE GAP, GRANDE MARAIS. FARM O 2 c 7 4 BREWERY I. 22 c.	
	19.4.17		No 1 3 & 4 Sections in the Trenches. Indirect fire carried out on FARM HOUSSAIN and LA BAS HAU.	
	20.4.17		No 2 Section relieved No 3 Section. Indirect fire carried out on FARM HOUSSAIN and LA BAS HAU	
	21.4.17		No 1 2 & 4 Sections in the Trenches.	
	22.4.17		No 1 2 & 4 Sections in the Trenches	
	23.4.17		No 1 2 & 4 Sections in the Trenches.	

2449 Wt. W14957/M90 750,000 1/16 J.B.C. & A. Forms/C.2118/12.

Instructions regarding War Diaries and Intelligence Summaries are contained in F. S. Regs., Part II. and the Staff Manual respectively. Title Pages will be prepared in manuscript.

WAR DIARY or INTELLIGENCE SUMMARY

(Erase heading not required.)

Army Form C. 2118.

172 Machine Gun Company

Place	Date	Hour	Summary of Events and Information	Remarks and references to Appendices
BOIS GRENIER	24.4.17		No 1 2 & 4 Sections in the Trenches.	
	25.4.17		No 1 2 & 4 Sections in the Trenches. The Company took over in addition to the BOIS GRENIER Sector the Machine gun defences of the RUE DU BOIS Sector from 173rd Machine Gun Company. Relief completed 11 pm. No 3 Section relieved No 4 Section	See Appendix III
BOIS GRENIER & RUE DU BOIS	26.4.17		No 1 2 & 3 Sections in the Trenches.	
	27.4.17		No 1 2 & 3 Sections in the Trenches	
	28.4.17		No 1 2 & 3 Sections in the Trenches	
	29.4.17		No 1 2 & 3 Sections in the Trenches.	
	30.4.17		No 1 2 & 3 Sections in the Trenches. Strength of Company on this date 197 – 10 Officers 180 O.R. and 7 attached Signallers	

2449 Wt. W14957/M90 750,000 1/16 J.B.C. & A. Forms/C.2118/12.

SECRET

Copy No. 6.

Appendix I

Operation Order No 1.
by
Capt. G. A. Wade
Commanding 172 Machine Gun Company.

In the field.

Ref. 1/10000 map 36 NW 4.

INFORMATION (1) Latest air photographs show signs of increased enemy activity in Square I 31 d.

INTENTION (2) An infantry party will raid enemy trenches at INCREASE I31d 8359 and will penetrate to I32c 0037 with object of procuring identifications and destroying personnel.
A box barrage will be formed by artillery, trench mortars and machine guns.

MACHINE GUNS (3) At Zero hour machine guns will open fire as under and continue firing till Zero + 30 minutes at the rate of half a belt per minute. From Zero + 30 minutes fire will gradually die down, ceasing at Zero + 35 minutes.
Guns will remain in position till Zero + 90 minutes ready to put down a further barrage if called for, or if artillery puts down another barrage.
After Zero + 90 minutes guns will take up their usual night lines
Section officers will make their own arrangements for S.A.A., Water, and Oil supply. All guns will have depression stops and section officers will personally supervise the laying of guns and adjustment of depression stops.
When guns are traversing, traversing stops will be arranged.
Guns will be laid and ready for firing at Zero - 30 mins.

ZERO. (4) Zero hour will be 10:25 p.m. 10/4/17.

P.T.O

(5)

Section	Gun	Position	Direction, Grid Bearing	Range	Elevation	Distance to Own Troops	Clearance
1	Reserve A	H24c 7612	132½°	2350	6° 20′	350 – 1900	36" – 84"
1	Reserve B	H24c 7913	133°	2350	6° 20′	350 – 1900	36" – 84"
1	Reserve C	H24c 8214	133°	2300	6°	350 – 1800	35" – 83"
1	Reserve D	H24c 8715	132½° 134°	2500	7° 27′	350 – 1900	44" – 121"
2	S4	H30b 6209	182°	2000	4° 16′	450 – 1250	30" – 59"
2	S11	I19d 1248	180°	2100	4° 48′	500 – 1500	38" – 65"
2	S12	I19d 1275	185°	2300	6°	750 – 1750	70" – 87"
3	R1.	H30d 3209 (I)	129°	1950	4° 1′	400 – 1100	26" – 53"
4	R5	I25b 7125 (M)	180° 186°	1900	3° 47′	500 – 1350	30" – 46"
~~4~~	~~R7~~	~~[illegible]~~	~~[illegible]~~	~~[illegible]~~	~~[illegible]~~	~~[illegible]~~	~~[illegible]~~
4	R8	I20c 1546 (P)	187°	1800	3° 21′	500 – 950	26" – 39"

REPORTS (6) Reports to O.C Barrage at CEMETERY DUGOUT. H30b6.5.

(7) Acknowledge.

G. A. Wade
Capt.
O.C 172 M.G.Coy

Issued 12 noon.

No 2 to OC No. 1 Sect
" 3 " " " 2
" 4 " " " 3
" 5 " " " 4
" 1 retained for O.C file
" 6 War Diary
" 7 } Spare.
" 8 }

Secret
Hospice Farm
The Brewery
Shaftesbury House
Bois-Grenier
Cemetery
Girls School
Shaftesbury Avenue
Tramline Avenue
30
25
London Bridge
Oxford Circus
Haymarket
Regent Street
Grande Flamengrie Fm
Moat Farm Ave
White City
Brewery
Touquet des Mages Femmes
36
The Temple
31
Water Farm
Blanco Ho
Rue des Bois Blancs
Oyster F
le Bridoux
Fme Houssein
White House
Datum House
H
I
N
O
172 Machine Gun Company
Scale 1.10,000
Approximate map
The fields of fire of several guns were altered after above map was made.
Capt.
172 MACHINE GUN COMPANY
ORDERLY ROOM
G.A.W817
Date 1/4/17.
MACHINE GUN CORPS

172 Machine Gun Company

10.4.17

Appendix I

Raid. – The enemy's trenches were entered and found to be held in strength. Raiding party came under heavy fire from rifles, rifle grenades and bombs and could make but slow progress on account of the resistance of the enemy generally, particularly from continued fire at short range from the support line and flanks. The use of a rifle grenade barrage by the enemy from the trenches in immediate rear and on the flanks of the front breastwork was most effective. The Infantry withdrew at the appointed time but were unable to bring back any prisoners or obtain any identifications. The enemy's artillery barrage was put down on N.M.L and our front and support lines within two minutes of zero. These trenches have been known for some time to be occupied by the enemy, but not in such strength as they were found on ~~this~~ night. The enemy made considerable use of very Bright rockets and many Very lights. Although the enemy was found in strength he made no attempt to follow up the retirement of our party nor did he employ much M.G. fire.

Operation Order No. 2

By Capt. G. A. Wade, commanding 172 Machine Gun Coy

Ref. Map 36 N.W.4 1/10,000. In the field 16/4/17.

INFORMATION. (1). Signs of enemy activity have been observed at about I 26 c 9.

INTENTION. (2). An infantry raiding party will enter trenches between I 26 c 80.00 & I 26 d 00.20 to a depth of 50 yards with object of destroying enemy work & personnel & getting identifications. A box barrage will be formed by Machine Guns, Artillery & Trench Mortars.

MACHINE GUNS. (3). Machine Guns will co-operate :-

170 M.G. Coy 4 guns
171 do 10 guns
172 do 10 guns
173 do 8 guns

(a) by barraging enemy front line on either flank of the raid for a distance of approximately 500 yards

(b). by barraging CTs running from I 32 a 70.70 to I 32 b 30.50 & from I 26 d 20.50 to I 26 d 35.15.

Objectives.. Objectives for guns of this company shown in Appendix A (back hereof)

Stops. All guns will have depression stops & traversing stops fitted before opening fire.

Fire. Guns will open fire at Zero hour & continue to fire till Zero + 25 min. remaining in position till Zero + 90 minutes ready to put down a further barrage if ordered, or if artillery does so.
Cue for putting down barrage at Zero will be taken from artillery.

Zero. Zero hour will be notified later.
After Zero + 90 minutes guns will take up their usual night lines.

S.A.A. Water & oil. O.C. Sections will arrange to have in all 10,000 K or KN S.A.A. with each gun & an adequate supply of water & oil.

REPORTS. (4). O.C. Barrage will be at BOIS GRENIER in 172 and 170 Coy's Battle HQ. (No. 1 Section's Officers dugout H 30 b 55.80.)

(5) Acknowledge.

Issued 12 noon.
No. 2 Copies to O.C. No. 1 Sect.
No. 3 Copy to O.C. No. 2 Sect.
" 4 " " " " 3 "
" 5 " " " " 4 "
" 1 " retained for operation order file
" 6 " " " letter diary.
" 7 }
" 8 } Spare

G. A. Wade
Capt
O.C. 172 M. G. Coy

Section	Gun	Position	Target	Direction	Elevation	Range.
2	Res A.	H24c75.11	I32a8664	121° grid	6°41'	2400.
2	" B.	H24c80.12	I32b0060	121° "	7°4'	2450.
2	" C.	H24c8214	I32b1060	121° "	7°27'	2500.
3	S1.	H30d08.52	I26d75.99	84¾° "	6°30'	2350.
3	R1.	H30d09.47	I26d6888	85¼° "	6°	2300.
3	R2.	H30d16.38	I26d6895	83° "	5°41'	2250.
3	J.	H30d22.32	I26b7008	81° "	6°	2300.
1	S4	(c) H30b06.00	I26d0998	91° "	6°20'	2350.
1	S11	I30a0120	I32a48.12.	174° "	4°32'	2050.
1	S12	I30a0620	I32a50.22	174° "	4°16'	2000.

172 Machine Gun Company

Appendix II

The Trenches were raided by 60 men of the 171st Brigade. Artillery reinforced. 30 - 18 pdrs 12 howitzers supporting infantry and 30 Machine guns put down a box barrage of frontal fire. Wire found well cut. Enemy line entered and found to be filled with wire. A small party of enemy was met, bombing ensued and the enemy was forced back up an island traversed trench. A dug out was bombed and a M G similar to a "Hotchkiss" reported destroyed. Enemys trench reported in good condition. The trench appears to be organized solely for defence. Enemy retaliation was weak. No prisoners were taken and no identifications obtained. Some casualties known to have been inflicted on the enemy. Casualties among our Infantry were 2 O R killed and 5 wounded. Fire of our artillery and our Machine guns reported excellent.

Operation Order No 3.

No map available

By Capt. G.A. Wade.

Commdg. 172nd Machine Gun Company

Ref. Map 36 N.W. 4 1/10,000.

In the Field 24/4/17

INFORMATION. On 25th Apl 1917 this company will take over, in addition to the BOIS GRENIER sector, the Machine Gun defences of the RUE DU BOIS sector from 173rd. Machine Gun Company.

INTENTION. The sixteen guns of this company will always be in position, as shown in attached SECRET map; but to enable the present system of one

MACHINE GUNS section being always in reserve, four of the guns (2, 9, 10, 11) will be manned by skeleton teams furnished by Nos 1, 2 & 3 Sections in the line.

One NCO & 4 men from each of Nos 1, 2 & 3 Sections will report to Lt Dyogan at LONDON BRIDGE at 3:0 pm. Lieut Dyogan will organize these men into gun teams & with them relieve teams of No. 4 Section at 2, 9, 10, 11. as soon as possible. O.C. No. 4 Section will hand over to Lt Dyogan, & obtain receipt for all his guns, tripods, belts & trench stores etc. After relief No. 4 Section will proceed to Coy. H.Q. Before 10 am. the team of No. 1 Section now at 2 will change over with team of No. 4 Section now at 3 (dugout near R8). Guns etc remaining where they are. Therefore before relief by skeleton teams No. 4 Section will be at 2, 9, 10, 11.

The teams of No. 1 Section at S.4, S5, S11 will proceed, taking as much of their gun material & equipment as possible, to PARK ROW where they will meet guides of 173rd M.G. Coy at 11 am. These guides will conduct them to the emplacements they are to occupy as under:-

Team from:-	To No. of emp. on map:-	No. given to emp by 173 Coy
S4.	4	11
S5.	5	11a
S11.	12	5

On arrival their material will be dumped, under guard of this company, & the teams will fetch remainder of belt boxes etc from old emplacements.

S.A.A. at S.4, S5, & S11 will be left there neatly stacked, ready to be fetched if required any time.

O.C. No. 3 Section will arrange with Transport Officer to have mules for his limbers sent to Coy HQ at 7:15pm. He will proceed with his men & guns to HQ 173rd M.G Coy at H 6d 75.80 arriving there at 8:30pm., not before. Guides will be furnished by O.C. 173 M.G. Coy to conduct teams of No 3 Section to 6.13.14.15 Emps. These emplacements are known to 173rd Coy as 12, 6, 9, 9a respectively

O.C No 173 M.G. Coy will then withdraw his guns from RUE DU BOIS sector & command of machine gun defence of RUE DU BOIS sector will pass to O.C 172 Coy.

O.C. No. 3 Section will arrange to take rations for 26th. Apl. as well as unexpended portion of rations for 25th. (if any)

CONTROL. For purposes of control the guns will be divided into four groups:-

A. — Yellow on map	1, 7, 8, 16.	2Lt. Donaldson	HQ	GREATWOOD AVENUE
B. — Orange	2, 3, 9, 10, 11.	" Vyvyan	"	LONDON BRIDGE
C. — Green	4, 5, 12.	" Ackroyd	"	Subsidiary Line Left of PARK ROW
D. — Blue.	6, 13, 14, 15.	" Gudd	"	LILLE POST.

In future when a section is relieved by another section the relieving section will also relieve men of that section in skeleton teams so that the section in reserve is complete.

By day 1 sentry, by night two sentries will be provided by skeleton teams at 9, 10 and 11, 13. between the two teams. Team at 2 will not provide sentries if arrangements can be made by O.C B Group for infantry to pass alarm to them in case of attack or gas.

Officers & N.C.Os must be particularly careful only to sign for what is actually handed over.

All emplacements & dugouts must be left spotlessly clean.

REPORTS To Coy HQ when relief complete.

By runner 12 midnight 24/25 Apl 1917.

Copy No. 1 to O.C. 172 M.G Coy.
" " 2 " O.C. No. 1 Sect
" " 3 " " " 2 "
" " 4 " " " 3 "
" " 5 " " " 4 "
" " 6 " C.S.M.
" " 7 " War Diary.
" " 8 " O.C 173 M.G Coy
" " 9 " 2Lt. Vyvyan.
" 10-12 Spare.

G.A. Wade
Capt.
O.C. 172 M.G. Coy.

Instructions regarding War Diaries and Intelligence Summaries are contained in F. S. Regs., Part II. and the Staff Manual respectively. Title Pages will be prepared in manuscript.

WAR DIARY
or
~~INTELLIGENCE SUMMARY~~
(Erase heading not required.)

Army Form C. 2118.

Original

142 Machine Gun Company.

Vol 4

Place	Date	Hour	Summary of Events and Information	Remarks and references to Appendices
RUE DU BOIS and BOIS GRENIER Sectors.	1.5.17.		Nos 1, 3 & 4 Sections in the trenches	
	2.5.17.		Nos 1, 3 & 4 Sections in the trenches. 12 O.R. reported.	
	3.5.17		Nos 1, 3 & 4 Sections in the trenches	
	4.5.17		No 4 Section relieved No 1 section.	
	5.5.17		Nos 2, 3 & 4 Sections in the trenches 2/Lt. E.W. Barber reported.	
	6.5.17		Nos 2, 3 & 4 Sections in the trenches	
	7.5.17		Nos 2, 3 & 4 Sections in the trenches. 1 O.R. wounded.	
	8.5.17		Nos 2, 3 & 4 Sections in the trenches	
	9.5.17		Nos 2, 3 & 4 Sections in the trenches Indirect fire carried out on FARM [O2c 74 (Sheet 36)] and on the ROAD near BATTERY HOUSE. [O2c 23 (Sheet 36)]	
	10.5.17		Nos 2, 3 & 4 Sections in the trenches. Indirect fire carried out on ROAD near BATTERY HOUSE [O2c 23 (Sheet 36)]; and LE BRIDOUX [O1b 37 (Sheet 36)]	
	11.5.17		No 1 Section relieved No 2 Section.	
	12.5.17		Nos 1, 3 & 4 Sections in the trenches.	
	13.5.17		Nos 1, 3 & 4 Sections in the trenches	
	14.5.17		Nos 1, 3 & 4 Sections in the trenches. Indirect fire carried out on CROSS ROADS at WEZ MACQUART [I22b 9580 (Sheet 36)]; DISTILLERY ROAD [I22d & b (Sheet 36)], and FLEUR D'ECOSSE [I29a 13 (Sheet 36)]	

2449 Wt. W14957/M90 750,000 1/16 J.B.C. & A. Forms/C.2118/12.

Instructions regarding War Diaries and Intelligence Summaries are contained in F. S. Regs., Part II. and the Staff Manual respectively. Title Pages will be prepared in manuscript.

WAR DIARY
or
~~INTELLIGENCE SUMMARY~~
(Erase heading not required.)

Army Form C. 2118.

Original
172 M. G. Coy

Place	Date	Hour	Summary of Events and Information	Remarks and references to Appendices
RUE DU BOIS and BOIS GRENIER Sector	15.5.17		Nos 1, 3 & 4 Sections in the trenches. Indirect fire carried out on the CROSS ROADS at WEZ MACQUART [I22b 9580 (Sheet 36)]; DISTILLERY ROAD [I22d & b (Sheet 36)] and FLEUR D'ECOSSE [I29a 13 (Sheet 36)].	
	16.5.17		Nos 1, 3 & 4 Sections in the trenches.	
	17.5.17		Nos 1, 3 & 4 Sections in the trenches.	
	18.5.17		No 2 Section relieved No 3 Section.	
	19.5.17		Nos 1, 2 & 4 Sections in the trenches.	
	20.5.17		Nos 1, 2 & 4 Sections in the trenches. Capt WADE left the company for a Machine Gun Course at CAMIERES.	
	21.5.17		Nos 1, 2 & 4 Sections in the trenches.	
	22.5.17		Nos 1, 2 & 4 Sections in the trenches.	
	23.5.17		Nos 1, 2 & 4 Sections in the trenches.	
	24.5.17		Nos 1, 2 & 4 Sections in the trenches.	
	25.5.17		No 3 Section relieved No 4 Section. Indirect fire was carried out on DISTILLERY ROAD [I22d & b (Sheet 36)]	
	26.5.17		Nos 1, 2 & 3 Sections in the trenches.	
	27.5.17		Nos 1, 2 & 3 Sections in the trenches.	
	28.5.17		Nos 1, 2 & 3 Sections in the trenches.	

2449 Wt. W14957/M90 750,000 1/16 J.B.C. & A. Forms/C.2118/12.

Army Form C. 2118.

Instructions regarding War Diaries and Intelligence Summaries are contained in F. S. Regs., Part II. and the Staff Manual respectively. Title Pages will be prepared in manuscript.

WAR DIARY
or
~~INTELLIGENCE~~ SUMMARY

(Erase heading not required.)

Original
142 M. G. Coy

Place	Date	Hour	Summary of Events and Information	Remarks and references to Appendices
RUE DU BOIS and BOIS GRENIER Sectors	29.5.17		Nos 1, 2 + 3 sections in the trenches. Indirect fire carried out on DISTILLERY ROAD (I 27 a and I 22 b + d [Sheet 36]). and GRANDE MARAIS [I 28 c 24 (Sheet 36)]	
	30.5.17		Nos 1, 2 + 3 sections in the trenches. Indirect fire carried out on DISTILLERY ROAD (I 27 a and I 22 b + d [Sheet 36]) and GRANDE MARAIS [I 28 c 24 (Sheet 36)].	
	31.5.17		Nos 1, 2 + 3 sections in the trenches.	

2449 Wt. W14957/M90 750,000 1/16 J.B.C. & A. Forms/C.2118/12.

Vol 5

War Diary

of

172nd Machine Gun Company.

Period

1st June 1917 to 30th June 1917

[illegible] Field
1.7.17.

Instructions regarding War Diaries and Intelligence Summaries are contained in F. S. Regs., Part II. and the Staff Manual respectively. Title Pages will be prepared in manuscript.

WAR DIARY
or
~~INTELLIGENCE SUMMARY~~

(Erase heading not required.)

Original.

Army Form C. 2118.

Place	Date	Hour	Summary of Events and Information	Remarks and references to Appendices
			Reference Maps Sheet 36 NW 4 (BOIS GRENIER) and Sheet 36 S W 2 (RADINGHEM) Scale 1:10,000 Edition 6 D. Scale 1:10000 Edition 6 D.	
RUE DU BOIS and BOIS GRENIER	1.6.17		No 4 Section relieved No 1 Section in the trenches. 1 O.R to Hospital. 5 O.R transferred to 173rd Machine Gun Company.	
	2.6.17		Nos 2,3 & 4 Sections in the trenches	
	3.6.17		Nos 2,3 & 4 Sections in the trenches	
	4.6.17		Nos 2,3 & 4 Sections in the trenches. 1 O.R to Hospital. 1 O.R to course with the 57th Divisional Train.	
	5.6.17		Nos 2,3 & 4 Sections in the trenches. Indirect fire carried out on DISTILLERY ROAD (I22b) and Gap in Enemy wire at I21b 9530.	
	6.6.17		Nos 2,3 & 4 Sections in the trenches. 8 O.R. transferred to 202nd Machine Gun Company. Indirect fire carried out on DISTILLERY ROAD at I22b; ROAD near BATTERY HOUSE (O2c2530) Gap in Enemy Wire at I21b 9530.	
	7.6.17		Nos 2,3 & 4 Sections in the trenches. 3 O.R. to Hospital. 3 O.R. to course in Anti aircraft gunnery.	
	8.6.17		No 1 Section relieved No 2 Section in the trenches. Capt G.A. WADE and 3 O.R returned from course at CAMIERES. Capt G.A. WADE resumed command of the Company.	

G.A. Wade Capt
O.C. 172 M.G. Coy

2449 Wt. W14957/M90 750,000 1/16 J.B.C. & A. Forms/C.2118/12.

Army Form C. 2118.

WAR DIARY
or
~~INTELLIGENCE SUMMARY~~
(Erase heading not required.)

Original

Instructions regarding War Diaries and Intelligence Summaries are contained in F. S. Regs., Part II. and the Staff Manual respectively. Title Pages will be prepared in manuscript.

Place	Date	Hour	Summary of Events and Information	Remarks and references to Appendices
RUE DU BOIS and BOIS GRENIER.	9.6.17		Nos 1, 3 & 4 Sections in the trenches. LT. C.M. HOWARD and 2 O.R. to Machine Gun Course at CAMIERES 1 O.R. returned from A.S.C. to duty with Company. 2 O.R. to Hospital. Indirect fire carried out on DISTILLERY ROAD (I22b); FLEUR D'ECOSSE (I29a 22); LE BAS HAU (O2d 16); Fme HOUSSAIN (O2a 47); THE GAP (O2b 40); LARGE FARM (I22c 59); CROSS ROADS at WEZ MACQUART (I23 a 08)	
	10.6.17		No 2 Section went into the trenches. 1 O.R. to hospital. 2 O.R. from Base as reinforcements. Indirect fire carried out on Fme HOUSSAIN (O2a 47), LE BAS HAU (O2d 16), THE GAP (O2b 40) GRANDE MAISNIL Fme (I33d 02), FLEUR D'ECOSSE (I29a 22), DISTILLERY ROAD (I22b).	
	11.6.17		Nos 1, 2, 3 & 4 Sections in the trenches. Operation Order No 4 issued. Indirect fire carried out on Fme HOUSSAIN (O2a 47); DISTILLERY ROAD (I22b); LE BAS HAU (O2d 16); THE GAP (O2b 40); Gd MAISNIL Fm (I33d 03); Enemy wire at I22a 47.	See Appendix I.
	12.6.17		Nos 1, 2, 3 & 4 Sections in the trenches. 2 O.R. arrived from hospital. Indirect fire carried out on RUELLE DE LA NOIX (I17b 21); FLEUR D'ECOSSE (I29a 22) LE BAS HAU (O2d 16), THE GAP (O2b 40). Direct fire on Enemy wire at I22a 44.	

2449 Wt. W14957/M90 750,000 1/16 J.B.C. & A. Forms/C.2118/12.

Army Form C. 2118.

Instructions regarding War Diaries and Intelligence Summaries are contained in F. S. Regs., Part II. and the Staff Manual respectively. Title Pages will be prepared in manuscript.

WAR DIARY
or
~~INTELLIGENCE SUMMARY~~
(Erase heading not required.)

Original

Place	Date	Hour	Summary of Events and Information	Remarks and references to Appendices
RUE DU BOIS and BOIS GRENIER	13.6.17		Nos 1, 2, 3 & 4 Sections in the trenches. 1 O.R. to BUSNES as witness on Field General Court Martial. Direct fire on gaps in Enemy Wire at I22a 4565; I22a 1240 and I21d 0075. Indirect fire carried out on Gd MAISNIL Fm (I33d 03); Fme HOUSSAIN (O2a 47); LE BAS HAV (O2d 16); GRAND MARAIS (I28c 24); LARGE FARM (I22c 59);	
	14.6.17		Nos 1, 2, 3 & 4 Sections in the trenches. 8 O.R. attached from 172 Inf. Bde for Rations only. 1 O.R. arrived from hospital. Direct fire on Gaps in Enemy wire at I22a 1240; I22a 4865 and I16d 2038. Indirect fire carried out on ROAD near MONT PINDO (I34a 34), Gd MAISNIL Fm (I33d 03) DISTILLERY ROAD (I22 b, d & c); LE BAS HAV (O2d 16); ROAD (I33d 13).	
	15.6.17		Nos 1, 2, 3 & 4 Sections in the trenches Direct fire on ~~I21d00~~ enemy wire at I21d 0075, I21b 8553, I22a 1240 and I16d 2038 in connection with a raid carried out by the 2/4th S. Lan R. Indirect fire on Fme HOUSSAIN (O2a 47) and LE BAS HAV (O2d 16). Operation Order No 5 issued	See Appendix I
	16.6.17		Nos 1, 2, 3 & 4 Sections in the trenches 1 O.R. returned from BUSNES. Indirect fire carried out on Gd MAISNIL Fm (I33d 03); RUELLE DE LA NOIX (I17b 21) LE BAS HAV (O2d 16), The GAP (O2b 40) and ROAD (I33d 15).	

2449 Wt. W14957/M90 750,000 1/16 J.B.C. & A. Forms/C.2118/12.

Army Form C. 2118.

WAR DIARY
or
~~INTELLIGENCE SUMMARY~~
(Erase heading not required.)

Original

Instructions regarding War Diaries and Intelligence Summaries are contained in F. S. Regs., Part II. and the Staff Manual respectively. Title Pages will be prepared in manuscript.

Place	Date	Hour	Summary of Events and Information	Remarks and references to Appendices
RUE DU BOIS AND BOISGRENIER	17.6.17.		Nos 1, 2, 3 & 4 Sections in the trenches. Indirect fire carried out on WEZ MACQUART (I23a 08); G^D MAISNIL F^M (I33d 03); F^ME HOUSSAIN (O2a 47); LE QUESNE (I33a 6595); DISTILLERY ROAD (I22 b d+c); PARADISE ROAD (I22d); THE GAP (O2b40); FARM (O2c 74); BAS MAISNIL (N12a 86) LE BAS HAU (O2d 16); CHATEAU RICHE (N11d 58).	
	18.6.17		Nos 1, 2, 3 & 4 Sections in the trenches. Indirect fire carried out on TRACKS at I23c93; DISTILLERY ROAD (I22 b d+c) by day: on CHATEAU D'HANCARDERIE (I23c 81); DUMP at I24c11; TRACKS at I23c93, ROAD S.E. of WEZ MACQUART (I23a); G^D MAISNIL F^M (I33d 03), PETIT MARAIS (I24b70), GRAND MARAIS (I28c 24), FARM (O2c74), BAS MAISNIL (N12a86); ROAD JUNCTION (N12b 5018) by night.	
	19.6.17		Nos 1, 2, 3 & 4 Sections in the trenches. 1 O.R. to Rest Camp First Army. Indirect fire carried out on TRACKS at I23c93; DISTILLERY ROAD (I22 b d+c); BREWERY (I22c 94); CHATEAU D'HANCARDERIE (I23c81) and DISTILLERY (I24b55) by day; and on TRACKS at I23c93, WEZ MACQUART (I23a 08); G^D MAISNIL F^M (I33d 03) DISTILLERY ROAD (I22 b d+c) and THE GAP (O2b40) by night.	
	20.6.17		Nos 1, 2, 3 & 4 Sections in the trenches 1 O.R accidentally wounded Indirect fire carried out on DISTILLERY RD (I22, 28 + 24) by day; and on WEZ MACQUART (I23a 08); ROADS + HOUSE in I34c; ROAD (I24c 94); LE QUESNE (I33a 6595) by night Direct fire was used against hostile aircraft during daylight	

2449 Wt. W14957/M90 750,000 1/16 J.B.C. & A. Forms/C.2118/12.

Army Form C. 2118.

Instructions regarding War Diaries and Intelligence Summaries are contained in F. S. Regs., Part II. and the Staff Manual respectively. Title Pages will be prepared in manuscript.

WAR DIARY
or
~~INTELLIGENCE SUMMARY~~

(Erase heading not required.)

Original

Place	Date	Hour	Summary of Events and Information	Remarks and references to Appendices
RUE DU BOIS AND BOIS GRENIER	21.6.17		Nos 1, 2, 3 + 4 Sections in the trenches. 1 O.R. from Base. Indirect fire was directed on Tracks at I23c93 and ROAD I24c94 by day; and on DUMP (I28c 8540) DISTILLERY ROAD (I22, 28 + 27); WEZ MACQUART (I23a 08); CHATEAU D'HANCARDRY (I23c 81); CHATEAU RICHE (N11d 58); THE GAP (O2b 40) by night.	
	22.6.17		Nos 1, 2, 3 + 4 Sections in the trenches. 1 O.R from Hospital. Hostile aircraft were engaged by direct fire during the day. Indirect fire was carried out at night against LA MOTTE HOUSSAIN Fm (I32d 15); DUMP (I28c 8540); DISTILLERY ROAD (I22, 28 + 24) Tracks at I23c93; ROAD S.E. of WEZ MACQUART (I23a); FARM (O2c 74); ROAD NEAR BATTERY HOUSE (O2c 33); THE GAP (O2b 40); BATTN H.Q. and ROAD (O4a 44); CHATEAU RICHE (N11d 58)	
	23.6.17		Nos 1, 2, 3 + 4 Sections in the trenches. 1 O.R returned from Hospital. 2 O.R to BUSNES as escort. Indirect fire was carried out on Tracks at I23c93; DISTILLERY ROAD (I22, 28 + 27) by day; and on LARGE FARM (I22c 59); INCIDENT ALLEY (I22b); TRACKS (I23c 93); ROAD S.E of WEZ MACQUART (I23a); BACQUART (O4a 96); THE GAP (O2b 40); DUMP (I21c 11); RICKS FOLLY (O4b 49) by night.	
	24.6.17		Nos 1, 2, 3 + 4 Sections in the trenches. Hostile aeroplanes were engaged during the day. Indirect fire was carried out on TRACKS (I23c93) by day; and on WEZ MACQUART (I23a 08); INCOMPLETE TRENCH (I26d); TRACKS (I23c 93) THE GAP (O2b 40); ROAD JUNCTION (N12b 5015); BAS MAISNIL (N12a 86); LE BAS HAV (O2d 16); and THE BREWERY (I22c 94) by night.	

2449 Wt. W14957/M90 750,000 1/16 J.B.C. & A. Forms/C.2118/12.

WAR DIARY
or
~~INTELLIGENCE SUMMARY~~

(Erase heading not required.)

Army Form C. 2118.

Instructions regarding War Diaries and Intelligence Summaries are contained in F. S. Regs., Part II. and the Staff Manual respectively. Title Pages will be prepared in manuscript.

Original

Place	Date	Hour	Summary of Events and Information	Remarks and references to Appendices
RUE DU BOIS AND BOIS GRENIER	25.6.17		Nos 1, 2, 3 & 4 Sections in the trenches. TRACKS at I23c 93 were fired on by day. Indirect fire carried out on LARGE FARM (I22c 59) PETIT MARAIS (I24b 70); ROAD S.E of WEZ MACQUART (I23a); TRACKS (I23c 93); BREWERY (I22c 94); LE GRAND MAISNIL F^m^ (I33d 03); DUMP (I24c 11), and RICK'S FOLLY (O 7b 49) by night. Hostile aircraft engaged by direct fire during daylight.	
	26.6.17		Nos 1, 2, 3 & 4 Sections in the Trenches. 3 O.R. returned from BUSNES. Operation Order No 6 issued. Indirect fire carried out on TRACKS (I23c) by day; and on BREWERY (I22c 94), TRACKS to DISTILLERY (I24b), DISTILLERY ROAD (I22, 28 & 24); BACQUART (O 4a 96); LE G^d^ MAISNIL F^m^ (I33d 03) and DUMP at I24c 11 by night.	See Appendix III
	27.6.17		Nos 1, 2, 3 & 4 Sections in the trenches. 1 O.R to BUSNES. 2 O.R arrived from BASE, 3 O.R arrived from A.A Course. Indirect fire was carried out by night on DISTILLERY (I 24b 55), LA HOUSSOIE (I24b 11); INCLEMENT SUPPORT (I22a), DUMP (I24c 11); ROAD AND WEZ MACQUART (I 23 a 08); ROAD S.E. of WEZ MACQUART (I23a) and Tracks (I23c 93) HOTEL at LA HOUSSOIE (I24d 88)	
	28.6.17		Nos 1, 2, 3 & 4 Sections in the trenches. Hostile aircraft engaged by fire during daylight. Indirect fire carried out on LARGE FARM (I22c 59) DISTILLERY ROAD (I22b, d + c); F^me^ DE L'EPERONNERIE (I23d 09); TRAMWAY (I22a); DISTILLERY (I24b 55); LA HOUSSOIE (I24c 88), WEZ MACQUART (I23a 08); LE BAS HAU (O2d 16); BACQUART (O4a 96)	

2449 Wt. W14957/M90 750,000 1/16 J.B.C. & A. Forms/C.2118/12.

Instructions regarding War Diaries and Intelligence Summaries are contained in F. S. Regs., Part II. and the Staff Manual respectively. Title Pages will be prepared in manuscript.

WAR DIARY
or
INTELLIGENCE SUMMARY
(Erase heading not required.)

Original

Army Form C. 2118.

Place	Date	Hour	Summary of Events and Information	Remarks and references to Appendices
RUE DU BOIS AND BOIS GRENIER	29.6.17		Nos 1, 2, 3 + 4 Sections in the Trenches	
			1 OR from BASE.	
		3.5pm	Raid by 2/10th Kings Liverpool Regt.	See Appendix A.
			Indirect fire carried out at night against INCLEMENT SUPPORT (I22 a); DISTILLERY RD (I22 c d rb); LARGE FARM (I22c 5 9)	
	30.6.17		Nos 1, 2, 3 + 4 Sections in the Trenches.	
			1 Officer + 2 OR returned from Course at CAMIÈRES. 1 Officer and 3 OR to anti aircraft course. 1 OR to hospital wounded.	
			Indirect fire carried out at night on DISTILLERY ROAD (I22 c d rb); ROAD LARGE FARM to DISTILLERY ROAD (I22c); WEZ MACQUART (I23 a 0 8); LARGE FARM (I22 c 59), AREA between INCLEMENT TRENCH and INCLEMENT SUPPORT (I22a).	

APPENDIX II

SECRET.

Operation Order No.5.
by
Capt. G.A.Wade,
Commanding 172nd M. G. Coy.

M. G. H.Q. BOIS GRENIER SECTOR.
15/6/1917.

Map Ref. 36 N.W.4. 1:10,000.

INFORMATION. (1) Gaps in wire have been cut by T.M.B. and kept open by Vickers.

INTENTION. (2) The 2/4 Btn.S.L .R. will raid the enemy trenches tonight on right & left of RUE DU BOIS Salient. Each raid consists of 2 or more Assaulting Parties and a covering party.

Parties will leave our trenches at Zero hour and cross N.M.L.in single file, but before entry will close on their leader and force an entry closing with enemy without hesitation should he open fire. Lewis guns will be well forward with the parties.

Parties will remain in enemy trenches for at least 20 minutes before withdrawing.

Should no enemy be discovered within time leaders of parties will extend their search.

DISTRIBUTION.(3)

RIGHT RAID.

Capt.Fox will conduct operations from I.21.c.50.80 in communication with AD.Batt. H.Q. by phone.

Hearn's Party leaves our trenches at I. 21.c. 50.80 & will follow the railway and enter at I.21.c.72.30

Robinson's Party will leave our trenches at I.21.c.70.80 and enter at I.21.c.85.53.

Rhodes' Party will follow Robinson's Party and will cover the operations from a point in N.M.L.at I.21.c.70.80.paying particular attention to left flank.

In event of enemy attack on the flanks in N.M.L.this party will lie close till he has approached and then go for him with bayonet.

This party will cover the withdrawal of other parties before coming in.

LEFT RAID.

Capt.Glascott will conduct the operations from I.15.d.40.10. will be in communication with Btn. H.Q.and his raiding parties by phone & runner.

Smith's Party will leave our trenches at I.15.d. 45.10. and will move by route already reconnoitred to I.21.b.78.40.attacking a sentry post there. If sentry post is not there they will move to C.T. I.21.b.90. 28.

Fairclough's Party.will leave our trenches at I.15.d.50.20. and go to I.22.a.18.45.

Harding's Party will leave our trenches at I.16.c.10.60. and move to I.22.a.45.70. Should wind be favourable this party will make a smoke barrage to attract enemy towards North away from main operations.

Taylor's Party (covering party) will follow Fairclough's Party and proceed to I.21.b.90.70 in N.M.L. where it will extend to right covering assaulting parties till they have withdrawn.

EQUIPMENT.

(4) All ranks taking part black their faces etc. and wear a label on 3rd Button of Jacket which act as a distinguishing marks

(For information only)

MACHINE GUNS. Machine guns will fire intermittently all night as usual on gaps at:-

I.16.d.20.38. No. 3 Section.
I.22.a.77.85. No. 3 Section.

They will also fire usual bursts of fire on gaps at:-

I.22.a.45.65. No. 3 Section.
I.21.d.00.75. No. 1 Section.
I.22.a.12.40 No. 3 Section.
I.21.c.85.55. No. 1 Section.

until 10-45 p.m. when they will raise their elevation so that it is impossible to hit anyone in No Man's Land and fire usual bursts on enemy back areas, to give enemy impression that gap is still being fired on.

O.C. Nos. 1 and 3 Sections will make arrangements for above and have everything in position at 9-30 p.m. when O.C. will make a round.

SIGNALS. SO.S. Signals will be susp-ended during raid.

Signal for withdrawal of party will be blasts on whistle given by their leader.
Signal for a general withdrawal will be a successin of white parachute lights from Advanced Battn. H.Q.

MEDICAL. Advanced Dressing Stn. at Adv.Batt. H.Q. Wounded will be evacuated by WELLINGTON & WINE AV.

ZERO.

REPORTS. O.C.Coy. will be with O. C. 2/4 S.L.R. at Advanced Btn.H.Q. I.21.a.40.45 in support line between RUE DU BOIS C.T. & SALOP AV. A runner from each of 1 & 3 Sections will be sent there as soo n as guns are in position. These men must know theway to each section officer in Front Line.

(Sgd) G. A. WA DE. Capt.
O.C. 172 M.G.Coy.

Issue d at 5.30 pm.

Copies to:-
No. 1 War Diary.
2 "
3 OC.No.1 Section.
4 " No.2 Section.

APPENDIX III

Operation Order No. 6

Copy No. 8

By Capt. G. A. Hall

Commanding 178 Machine Gun Company

In the Field 22-10-17.

Ref. Maps.
Sheet 36 N.W.4 1:10000
" " S.W.2 1:10000
Special Map attached.

I. **INFORMATION.** Information gained by patrols show that trenches at INDEX and INCREASE are occupied. A prisoner who deserted from No5 Company 78th LANDWEHR REGIMENT on the 18th inst. confirms this. Each company has a Machine Gun in the Front Line and it is moved about and fired over the parapet at night. The majority of M.G. emplacements are in the support line. Salient at I31D01.85 is held by a Sentry Post

2. **INTENTION.** "C" Company of the 2/10th (Scottish) K.L.R. will raid the German Front Line Trench between points I.31.D.03.25 and I.31.C.90.10 and penetrate to his support line between points I.31.D.19.10 to O.1.A.99.91 with the object of destroying as many Germans as possible, taking a few prisoners for identification, destroying his defences, and bringing back booty.
Company Commander is Captain A. P. Dickinson. The raid in all further references will be called "DICKY'S DASH".

3. **GENERAL OUTLINE.** Raid will take place from the BRIDOUX SALIENT at zero hour on "Z" day under cover of Artillery barrage placed on enemy's front line from INCOMPLETE TRENCH to NEAR TRENCH with an intense bombardment of that portion of the enemy's front and support lines in which raiding party will enter.
The Artillery barrage will be strengthened on the flanks by Medium and Light Trench Mortars. There will also be a Machine Gun Box Barrage co-operating with that of Artillery.
The raiders will remain in the enemy's trenches until zero + 30 when the withdrawal from the Support Line will commence.
There will be a Smoke Cloud Discharge from our Front Line Trench at I.26.3 to I.26.4 to form a diversion when the raiders commence to withdraw from the enemy's trenches. Box Barrage will be formed

O.1.A 65.96 to O.1.A 80.72 — O.1.B.12.70 - O.1.B.25.61. — I.31.D 25.26. to I.31.D. 30.15

O.1.B 38.74 - O.1.B 10.90

Operation Order No 6 (contd)

Edges of box to be turned down along Front Line for at least 100 yards.

MACHINE GUNS.

Fourteen Guns will be detailed to intensify the Artillery Box Barrage and the remaining two will be placed in our Front Line on either flank of the raiding party:-

(A) To knock out any hostile Machine Guns firing on our Raiding Party over enemy parapet

(B) To prevent enemy attacking our party in No Mans Land

(C) To cover withdrawal when raid is completed.

The Barrage Guns will be divided into Batteries and assigned areas to barrage as under

No. of Battery	No of Guns	Present position of Guns	Section	Approximate position of Battery	Area to be barraged shown on attached Mapping	Officer
1	3	1, 7, 8	2	H.29.D 2.9	Yellow	Lt Donaldson W.G.
2	3	10.11.3	4	H 29.D 4.9	Red	Lt Jones E.E.
3	4	2, 4, 5, 6	1	I 19.D 3.7	Blue	Lt Ackroyd L.F.M.
4	4	12, 13, 14, 15	3	I 20a 3.0	Green	Lt Greenwood O.

As will be seen from the map, no bullets pass directly over raiding party. Of the Front Line Guns No 16 will be at about I 31.C. 00.15 and No 9 at about I 31.B 96. These Guns will be under 2/Lt Barker E.W. who will remain with Gun at I 31 B 96 during raid. They will be provided with Overbank Mountings and 2/Lt Barker will at once reconnoitre the Front Line to select positions. O.C No 4 Section will if necessary provide a working party to make the emplacements - at least two will be made for each gun. These guns will be in position and mounted at Zero - 45 minutes but will not be laid over parapet until occasion arises.

O.C Batteries will at once reconnoitre the positions, have platforms made and aiming posts laid out. The Guns will be relieved at Zero - 6 hours by Lewis Guns of Reserve Battalions and will then proceed to their Battery Positions. They must be laid and fitted with substantial depression stops at Zero - 1½ hours ready for inspection by O.C. Company. Direction must be obtained most accurately and must be checked in as many ways as possible. For details of direction and elevation see Appendix I and for particulars of Times and Rate of Fire Appendix II.

Operation Order No 6 (Contd)

10. INFANTRY ACTION.

(A) Jumping off trench for raiding party will be prepared in BRIDOUX Salient opposite front of enemy's trench to be raided.

(B) Infantry will move forward in two waves at Zero hour.

(C) As soon as the Barrage lifts from the Front Line the first wave will enter Enemy's Front Line Trench.

(D) At Zero + 7 the leading parties of the first wave will form blocks on the flanks and enter enemy's support line.

(E) At Zero + 30 troops in support line commence to withdraw.

11. SIGNALS for ARTILLERY and MACHINE GUNS.

In the event of it being found necessary through some unforseen contingency to postpone the operation and there not being time to communicate by telephone to the Batteries taking part a parachute rocket with a red smoke will be sent up from trench I.31.3 in our Front Line and repeated at Battalion Headquarters FLAMENGRIE SUBSECTOR I.19.B.7.1. This signal will mean that Z. ZO hour has been postponed for 60 minutes. If it is desired to cancel the operations altogether the Artillery and all concerned will be informed in that period by a code message.

12. CODE

The following Code Words will be used in connection with this operation:-

Operations postponed for 60 minutes.	CABBAGE.
Operations cancelled for the day.	POTATO.
Cease fire.	PARSLEY.
Party entering First Line.	MUSTARD.
Party entering Second Line.	CRESS.
All doing well.	CELERY.
Much resistance.	BEANS.
Reserve Platoon Required.	CAPERS.
WEAK RESISTANCE	PEAS.
Prisoners returning	SEEDS.
Many casualties	ONIONS.
Party returning	LETTUCE.
All in	ENDIVE.

13. COMMUNICATIONS

No's 1 and 3 Batteries will be connected by phone to right Battalion H.Q. In addition a runner from each Battery will be at right Battalion H.Q (RITZ)

Operation order No 6 (Contd)

at Zero – 45 minutes. 2/Lt Barber will also send a runner who knows the position of both his Guns, to be there at that time.

14. SYNCHRONIZATION OF WATCHES. Lieut Donaldson will obtain correct time from Brigade Intelligence Officer at MOAT FARM at Zero – 1½ hours.

15. ZERO. Zero day will be between the dates of June 28th and July 1st if Artillery is available.

16. ACKNOWLEDGE

Issued at by Runner

Copy No. 1. 172 Brigade
" 2 O.C. 2/10 Battalion Liverpool Regiment.
" 3 O.C. No. 1 Section
" 4 O.C. No. 2. "
" 5 O.C. No. 3 "
" 6 O.C. No 4
" 7. 2/Lieut. Barber.
" 8. War Diary. ×
" 9 }
" 10 } Kept.
" 11 }

G. A. Wade
Capt.
Commdg 172nd M. G. Coy.

Fire Instructions

Appendix I

Battery	Gun	Gun Position	Target	Grid Direction	Range	Elevation	Range to crest (Tracer) [illegible]		Clearances	
3	1	I18C 9970	01B3787	175½°	2450x	7° 4'	650x	1700x	62x	99x
	2	I19D 0175	01B3680	176°	2500x	7° 27'	700x	1900x	80	111x
	3	I19D 0578	[illegible]	176½°	2550x	7° 51'	750x	1950x	92x	121x
	4	I19D 0881	[illegible]	178½°	2600x	8° 16'	750x	1950x	99x	133x
4	1	I20A 2709	I31D4435	190°	2400x	6° 41'	600x	1700x	58x	87x
	2	I20A 3004	I31D4039	189°	2400x	6° 41'	600x	1900x	58x	87x
	3	I20A 3700	I31D4010	191°	2500x	7° 27'	600x	1900x	68x	111x
	4	I20C 5897	01B3374	191½°	2700x	9° 11'	550x	1850	82x	170x
1	1	H29D 0069	01A5790	130°	2400x	6° 41'	300x	2000x	33x	72x
	2	H29D 0391	01A7517	130½°	2450x	7° 4'	300x	2000x	35x	87x
	3	H29D 0693	01A9368	130°	2550x	7° 51'	300x	2000x	38x	115x
2	1	H29D 1297	01A9870	130½°	2550x	7° 51'	300x	2000x	38x	115x
	2	H29D 1599	01B3257	130°	2700x	9° 11'	300x	2000x	46x	162x
	3	H29B 1202	01B1567	130°	2600x	8° 15'	300x	2000x	40x	129x

APPENDIX II

TIME and RATE of FIRE.

(1) Zero + 1½ – Zero + 45 minutes .... Guns fire 50 100 rounds per minute

Zero + 45 – Zero + 50 .... Guns gradually cease fire

Zero + 50 – Zero + 80 .... Guns remain in position ready to put down a further barrage if called for or if Artillery suspends fire.

Zero + 80 .... Guns return to usual positions

(2). S.A.A., WATER AND OIL SUPPLY.

At each barrage gun position will be 16 Belts, 3 Boxes S.A.A., 1 Petrol tin water.

Handles will be filled with oil before guns leave emplacements and Section Officers will arrange for a reserve supply at each battery position. Tins of water and S.A.A.; also 2 belts per gun will be sent from Coy. H.Q.

APPENDIX III

Ref. O.O. No 6. following amendments are made:-

Para. 3. SMOKE. By agreement with and arrangements made by the 170th Infantry Brigade smoke candles will be provided in their front line trench at about N.6.c.65.35 should the wind be N.E. these will be fired instead of those provided for in Para. 3.

Para 11. SIGNALS Add "If the red smoke signal is fired after Zero it will mean that barrage will be maintained a further fifteen minutes."

Para 12. Add:

CODE. Continue Barrage till Zero + 65 .... LEEKS.

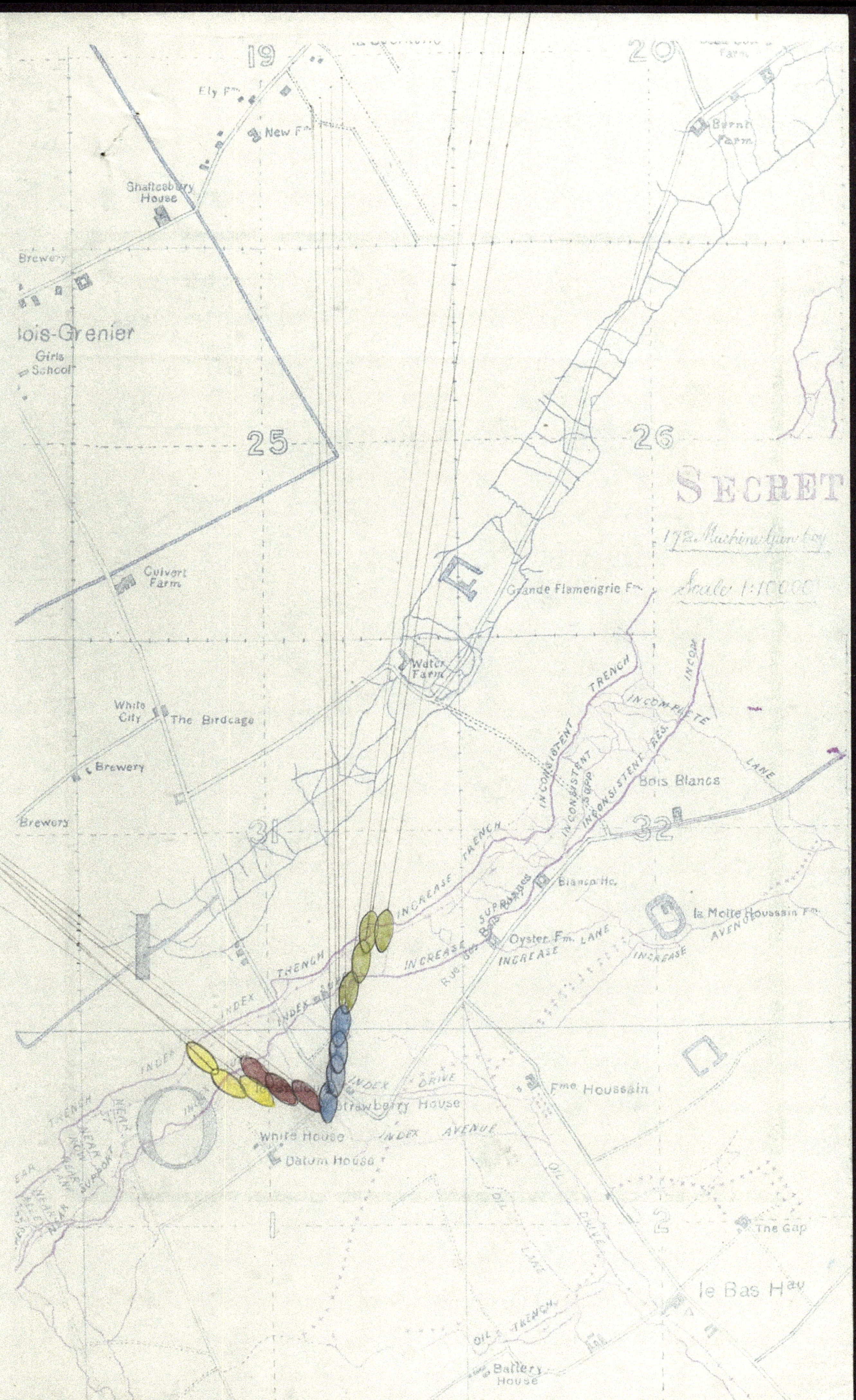

19
20
Ely Fm
New Fm
Bernt Farm
Shaftesbury House
Brewery
Bois-Grenier
Girls School
25
26
SECRET
17th Machine Gun Coy
Scale 1:10000
Culvert Farm
Grande Flamengrie Fm
Water Farm
White City
The Birdcage
Brewery
Brewery
TRENCH
INCOMPLETE
INCONSISTENT
INCONSISTENT SUPP
INCONSISTENT RES.
LANE
Bois Blancs
31
32
INCREASE TRENCH
Blanche Ho.
la Motte Houssain Fm
Oyster Fm.
INCREASE LANE
INCREASE AVENUE
INCREASE
INDEX TRENCH
INDEX DRIVE
Fme Houssain
Strawberry House
White House
INDEX AVENUE
Datum House
OIL DRIVE
OIL LANE
OIL TRENCH
2
The Gap
le Bas Hay
Battery House

172ND
MACHINE GUN
COMPANY.
No. H/15/1
Date 31/1/8/17

From O.C. 172 M.G. Coy
To D.A.G. 3rd Echelon Base.

Herewith duplicate War Diary of the above Company for July 1917.

C S H Gadd 2/Lt

for O.C. 172 Machine Gun Coy.

Army Form C. 2118.

Instructions regarding War Diaries and Intelligence Summaries are contained in F. S. Regs., Part II. and the Staff Manual respectively. Title Pages will be prepared in manuscript.

WAR DIARY
or
~~INTELLIGENCE SUMMARY~~

(Erase heading not required.)

172 M.G. Coy
Original Copy
Vol 6

Place	Date	Hour	Summary of Events and Information	Remarks and references to Appendices
			Reference TRENCH MAP - BOIS GRENIER Sheet 36 NW 4 Edition 6 D Scale 1:10,000 and TRENCH MAP - RADINGHEM Sheet 36 SW 2 Edition 6 D Scale 1:10,000.	
BOIS GRENIER and RUE DU BOIS Sectors.	1.7.17		Nos 1, 2, 3 & 4 Sections in the trenches 1 O.R. to M.G. Course at CAMIERES; 1 O.R. returned from BUSNES. Hostile aircraft engaged during the day. Indirect fire carried out by night on LARGE FARM (I22c59) QUEER ST. (I22a); QUEER ST to LA HOUSSOIE (I27b, I28a, I22c); ROAD near BATTERY HOUSE (O2c33) DISTILLERY ROAD (I22 c, d & b), INCLEMENT SUPPORT (I21b & I22a); CROSS ROADS WEZ MACQUART (I22b9580)	
	2.7.17		Nos 1, 2, 3 & 4 Sections in the trenches. Indirect fire carried out on LARGE FARM (I22c59); QUEER ST to LA HOUSSOIE (I27b, I28a, I22c) ROAD near BATTERY HOUSE (O2c33); DISTILLERY ROAD (I22c, d & b); INCLEMENT SUPPORT (I21b & I22a), and CROSS ROADS WEZ MACQUART (I22b9580)	
	3.7.17		Nos 1, 2, 3 & 4 Sections in the Trenches 1 O.R. to UK on leave; 1 O.R. to 1st Army Rest Camp. Indirect fire carried out on LARGE FARM (I22c59), QUEER ST. to LA HOUSSOIE (I27b, I28a, I22c) ROAD near BATTERY HOUSE (O2c33), DISTILLERY ROAD (I22c, d & b), INCLEMENT SUPPORT (I21b & I22a) and CROSS ROADS WEZ MACQUART (I22b9580).	
	4.7.17		Nos 1, 2, 3 & 4 Sections in the trenches 1 O.R. returned from Rest camp. Hostile aircraft engaged during the day. Indirect fire by night was carried out against DISTILLERY ROAD (I22c d & b); LARGE FARM to LA HOUSSOIE (I27b, I28a & I22c), INCLEMENT SUPPORT (I21b and I22a) and CROSS ROADS WEZ MACQUART (I22b9580).	

[illegible signature]
Capt.
Commdg 172nd M.G. Coy.

2449 Wt. W14957/M90 750,000 1/16 J.B.C. & A. Forms/C.2118/12.

Army Form C. 2118.

Instructions regarding War Diaries and Intelligence Summaries are contained in F. S. Regs., Part II. and the Staff Manual respectively. Title Pages will be prepared in manuscript.

WAR DIARY
or
~~INTELLIGENCE SUMMARY~~

(Erase heading not required.)

Original

Place	Date	Hour	Summary of Events and Information	Remarks and references to Appendices
BOIS GRENIER and RUE DU BOIS Sectors	5.7.17		Nos 1, 2, 3 & 4 Sections in the trenches 1 OR to Hospital Indirect fire carried out on LARGE FARM. (I22c59)	
	6.7.17		Nos 1, 2, 3 & 4 Sections in the trenches 1 O.R admitted to Hospital Fire directed on Snipers post in tree at O3b84. Indirect fire carried out by night on DISTILLERY ROAD (I22 c d & b), CROSS ROADS WEZ MACQUART (I22b9580), & LARGE FARM (I22c59)	
	7.7.17		Nos 1, 2, 3 & 4 Sections in the Trenches Indirect fire was directed on our FRONT LINE at I15d and No Mans Land and Enemy Front line in anticipation of a hostile raid. Fire was opened soon after the enemy barrage was put down. Indirect fire was also carried out on LARGE FARM (I22c59).	
	8.7.17		Nos 1, 2, 3 & 4 Sections in the trenches Indirect fire carried out on DISTILLERY ROAD (I 22 c, d & b).	
	9.7.17		Nos 1, 2, 3 & 4 Sections in the trenches. 1 OR wounded and admitted to hospital. Indirect fire was directed on DISTILLERY ROAD (I22c, d & b), INCIDENT ALLEY (I22b), LARGE FARM (I22c59), INCEMENT SWITCH (I22a) and ROAD (O3c1085) in cooperation with the 2/5th S. LANC. REGT who were raiding the enemy line at I22a 1545 1 OR returned from Course.	
	10.7.17		Nos 1, 2, 3 & 4 Sections in the trenches Hostile aircraft engaged during the day. Indirect fire was directed on DISTILLERY RD (I22c, d & b) by night	

2449 Wt. W14957/M90 750,000 1/16 J.B.C. & A. Forms/C.2118/12.

Instructions regarding War Diaries and Intelligence Summaries are contained in F. S. Regs., Part II. and the Staff Manual respectively. Title Pages will be prepared in manuscript.

WAR DIARY
or
~~INTELLIGENCE SUMMARY~~
(Erase heading not required.)

Army Form C. 2118.

Original

Place	Date	Hour	Summary of Events and Information	Remarks and references to Appendices
BOIS GRENIER AND RUE DU BOIS Sectors.	11.7.17.		Nos 1,2,3 & 4 Sections in the trenches	
			2 O.R to Hospital	
			Hostile aircraft engaged during the day.	
	12.7.17		Nos 1,2,3 & 4 Sections in the trenches	
			1 O.R to Hospital.	
	13.7.17		Nos 1,2,3 & 4 Sections in the trenches	
			Hostile aircraft engaged. Indirect fire was carried out on THE GAP (O2d 5095)	
	14.7.17		Nos 1,2,3 & 4 Sections in the trenches.	
			1 Officer left for U.K. on leave. Lt C.W. Howard assumed command of the company.	
			Hostile aircraft engaged during the day	
	15.7.17.		Nos 1,2,3 & 4 Sections in the trenches	
	16.7.17		Nos 1,2,3 & 4 Sections in the trenches.	
			1 O.R from hospital to duty	
			Hostile aircraft engaged.	
	17.7.17		Nos 1,2,3 & 4 Sections in the trenches.	
	18.7.17		Nos 1,2,3 & 4 Sections in the trenches	
			1 O.R to Hospital, 1 OR to Rest Camp; 1 OR from Rest Camp.	
			Indirect fire carried out on gap in Enemy wire (~~[illegible]~~) (I5d 2262 to I5c 8530)	
	19.7.17		Nos 1,2,3 & 4 Sections in the trenches	
			5 Reinforcements arrived from Base; 1 OR returned from leave.	
		11.30pm	Gas was projected into enemy lines near WEZ MACQUART.	
			Indirect fire carried out on gap in Enemy wire (I5c + d).	

Instructions regarding War Diaries and Intelligence Summaries are contained in F. S. Regs., Part II. and the Staff Manual respectively. Title Pages will be prepared in manuscript.

WAR DIARY
or
~~INTELLIGENCE SUMMARY~~
(Erase heading not required.)

Army Form C. 2118.

Original

Place	Date	Hour	Summary of Events and Information	Remarks and references to Appendices
BOIS GRENIER AND RUE DU BOIS SECTORS.	20.7.17		Nos 1,2,3 & 4 Sections in the ~~Line~~ Trenches 1 O.R to hospital ARMENTIERES heavily shelled by guns of all calibres throughout the night. Gas shells were used Carried out indirect fire on gap in Enemy wire at I5 c r d.	
	21.7.17		Nos 1,2,3 & 4 Sections in the trenches. Indirect fire on the gap in Enemy wire at I5 c r d carried out. Heavy ~~shellin~~ hostile shelling of ARMENTIERES continued	
	22.7.17		Nos 1,2,3 & 4 Sections in the trenches Indirect fire carried out on the gap in Enemy Wire at I5 c r d. Hostile planes engaged. Shelling of ARMENTIERES continued. 1 Officer to UK on leave.	
	23.7.17		Nos 1,2,3 & 4 Sections in the trenches 1 Officer and 3 O.R returned from ~~An~~ Anti aircraft Course Indirect fire carried out on the gap in Wire at I5 c r d. Enemy shelled our trenches with gas shells.	
	24.7.17		Nos 1,2,3 & 4 Sections in the Trenches. Gaps in enemy wire at I5 c r d, O1 a 5892 and O1 a 5090 fired upon. Hostile aircraft engaged. 2 O.R to hospital.	
	25.7.17		Nos 1,2,3 & 4 Sections in the Trenches 2 O.R to hospital	
	26.7.17		Nos 1,2,3 & 4 Sections in the Trenches. Indirect fire carried out on TRACKS (I23 c 93); ROAD LARGE FARM to DISTILLERY RD (I22 c); RUELLE DE LA NOIX (I17 c 31); FLEUR D'ECOSSE (I29 a 22); GRAND MAISNIL F^m (I33 d 02); INCIDENT ALLEY (I22 b); PARADISE ROAD (I22 d); THE GAP (O2 d 59); DUMP (I27 c 11); CHATEAU RICHE (N11 d 58)	

2449 Wt. W14957/M90 750,000 1/16 J.B.C. & A. Forms/C.2118/12.

Army Form C. 2118.

Instructions regarding War Diaries and Intelligence Summaries are contained in F. S. Regs., Part II. and the Staff Manual respectively. Title Pages will be prepared in manuscript.

WAR DIARY
or
~~INTELLIGENCE SUMMARY~~
(Erase heading not required.)

Original

Place	Date	Hour	Summary of Events and Information	Remarks and references to Appendices
RUE DU BOIS and BOIS GRENIER Sectors.	27.7.17		Nos 1, 2, 3 & 4 Sections in the trenches	
			3 OR to Antiaircraft course. 2 OR from Hospital; 1 OR from M.G. Course; 1 Officer from leave.	
			Capt GAWADE resumed command of the Company.	
			Indirect fire carried out on Fme DE L'EPPERONNERIE (I 23 c 99); ROAD LARGE FARM to DISTILLERY ROAD (I 22 c), FLEUR D'ECOSSE (I 29 a 22), DUMP (I 24 c 11); LE QUESNE (I 33 a 69) ROAD 08 b 88. Hostile planes engaged during the day.	
	28.7.17		Nos 1, 2, 3 & 4 Sections in the trenches.	
			Indirect fire carried out on DUMP (I 24 c 11); LE QUESNE (I 33 a 69); MONT PINDO (I 34 a); BREWERY (I 24 c)	
			New Defence Scheme came into operation.	
			Indirect fire was carried out on Fme de L'EPERRONNERIE (I 23 c 99); WEZ MACQUART (I 22 b) ESTAMINET DE LA BARRIERE (I 22 b 05); MONT PINDO (I 34 a); CH. D'HANCARDRY (I 23 c 08)	
	29.7.17		Nos ~~1~~ 2, 3 & 4 Sections in the trenches	
		2am–3am	Heavy bombardment of ARMENTIERES. Many gas shells were used many of which fell near H.Q. billets. Many fires were caused in the town.	
			The shelling of the town and H.Q. billets continued during the day. The Company had 24 casualties (O.R) from gas and 2 OR wounded.	
			The 2nd Battery Independent Machine Guns Heavy (2 B.I.M.P) of the PORTUGUESE Expeditionary forces were attached to the Company for instruction. Strength 178.	
			Indirect fire carried out on DISTILLERY RD (I 22 b c+d); Fme DE LA EPERRONNERIE (I 23 c 99); WEZ MACQUART (I 22 b); EST. DE LA BARRIERE (I 22 b 05); MONT PINDO (I 34 a) CHATEAU D'HANCARDRY (I 23 c 08)	

2449 Wt. W14957/M90 750,000 1/16 J.B.C. & A. Forms/C.2118/12.

Instructions regarding War Diaries and Intelligence Summaries are contained in F. S. Regs., Part II. and the Staff Manual respectively. Title Pages will be prepared in manuscript.

WAR DIARY
or
~~INTELLIGENCE SUMMARY~~
(Erase heading not required.)

Army Form C. 2118.

Original

Place	Date	Hour	Summary of Events and Information	Remarks and references to Appendices
BOIS GRENIER AND RUE DU BOIS SECTORS	30/7/17		Nos 2, 3 + 4 Sections in the trenches. There were a further 24 casualties resulting from the hostile gas bombardment. The HQ billet was again heavily shelled. The PORTUGUESE attached to the company suffered casualties 3 OR killed and 5 OR wounded. The HQ billet was removed to the BATHS ERQUINGHEM Indirect fire was carried out on the same targets as on the 29th.	
	31.7.17		Nos 2, 3 + 4 Sections in the trenches 1 O.R to Hospital (gas); 1 officer + 3 OR to 1st Army Rest Camp. 1 OR from hospital	
			Note: Civilians in ARMENTIERES suffered severely from new Poison Gas Shells, & can be seen about RUE MARLE blind leading blind in groups of six. A number of civilians refuse to move in spite of it all & in several cases old men & women remain suffering from gas in areas shelled severely, without food, & none apparently taking any interest in them. Most of the gas cases we had seemed slight but developed rapidly. Eyes chiefly being attacked. All cases however slight were taken to hospital.	

G. A. W[illegible]
Capt.
Commdg 172nd Inf. Coy

2449 Wt. W14957/M90 750,000 1/16 J.B.C. & A. Forms/C.2118/12.

4

To D.A.G.
3rd Echelon BASE.

172ND
MACHINE GUN
COMPANY.
No. H/19/6
Date. 1/9/17.

From O.C.
172nd Machine Gun Coy.

Herewith Original War Diary of this Company for August 1917 please.

O. Greenwood 2Lt.

for. O.C. 172 Machine Gun Coy.

Army Form C. 2118. 57

Instructions regarding War Diaries and Intelligence Summaries are contained in F. S. Regs., Part II. and the Staff Manual respectively. Title Pages will be prepared in manuscript.

WAR DIARY
or
~~INTELLIGENCE SUMMARY~~

(Erase heading not required.)

172 M G Coy
Vol 7

Place	Date	Hour	Summary of Events and Information	Remarks and references to Appendices
			Ref TRENCH MAP - BOIS GRENIER - Sheet 36 N.W.4 Edition 6D Scale 1:10,000 and TRENCH MAP - RADINGHEM - Sheet 36 S.W. 2 Edition 6D Scale 1:10,000.	
BOIS GRENIER and RUE du BOIS Sectors.	1.8.17	1-30AM	Four Officers and 133 O.R's of D Company 2/4th Batt South Lancs Regt raided the quadrilateral of the enemy trenches I22a 30.55; I22a 16.43; I22a 30.32; I22a 40.43; The Machine Guns cooperated by helping create a complete box barrage diversion round WEZ MACQUART. For particulars see APPENDIX attached. This diversion drew the greater part of the enemy artillery fire against CHARDS FARM SALIENT. The raiding party encountered but a thin and scattered barrage.	Machine Gun Operation Order attached and Numbered I.
			The raiding party captured 4 prisoners but only two reached our lines. At least 25 Germans were killed during the raid.	
			When our guns opened at the commencement of the raid one man of the PORTUGUESE Machine Gun Battery attached to this Company fell dead of heart failure.	
			Indirect fire carried out by night on LARGE FARM (I22c 5.9) DISTILLERY ROAD (I22c d+b); CROSS ROADS WEZ MACQUART (I22b 95 80); ESTAMINET D'la BARRIERE (I22b 05); HALT MONT PINDO (I34a); and Ch. D'HANCARDRY (I23c 08).	
	2.8.17		Nos 2, 3 and 4 Sections in the trenches.	
			Indirect fire carried out on HALT MONT PINDO (I34a); CH D'HANCARDRY (I23c 08); ESTAMINET DE LA BARRIERE (I22b 05); DISTILLERY ROAD (I22c, d+b);	

2449 Wt. W14957/M90 750,000 1/16 J.B.C. & A. Forms/C.2118/12.

Instructions regarding War Diaries and Intelligence Summaries are contained in F. S. Regs., Part II. and the Staff Manual respectively. Title Pages will be prepared in manuscript.

WAR DIARY
or
INTELLIGENCE SUMMARY
(Erase heading not required.)

Army Form C. 2118.

Place	Date	Hour	Summary of Events and Information	Remarks and references to Appendices
	2.8.17		CROSS ROADS WEZ MACQUART (I22b 95 80); ROAD-LARGE FARM (I22c); LE BAS HAU (O2d); and BACQUART (O4b).	
			1 Other rank admitted to hospital (gassed)	
			1 O.R. returned from 1st Army Rest Camp.	
	3.8.17		Numbers 2, 3 & 4 sections in the trenches.	
			Indirect fire carried out on ROAD-LARGE FARM (I22c); DISTILLERY ROAD (I22c d & b); ESTAMINET DE LA BARRIER (I22b 05); CROSS ROADS WEZ MACQUART (I22b 95 80); HALT MONT PINDO (I34a); CH. D'HANCARDRY (I23c 08):	
			2 O.R's admitted to hospital (1 gassed and 1 sick).	
			1 Officer returned from leave.	
	4.8.17		Numbers 2, 3 & 4 Sections in the trenches.	
			Indirect fire carried out on DUMP at INCOMPLETE TRENCH (I26d 75 55); THE GAP (O2d 5095); HALT MONT PINDO (I34a); BACQUART (O7b).	
			26 O.R. reinforcements reported from M.G.C. Base Depot	
	5.8.17		Numbers 2, 3 & 4 Sections in the trenches.	
			Indirect fire carried out on LE GRAND MAISNIL FARM (I33d); CHATEAU D' HANCARDRY (I23c 08); ROAD-LARGE FARM (I22c); DISTILLERY ROAD (I22c d & b); CROSS ROAD WEZ MACQUART (I22b 95 80); INCOMPLETE SUPPORT and AVENUE (I26d 72 52); THE GAP (O2d 5095); HALT MONT PINDO (I34a); BACQUART (O7b).	
			1 Officer to U.K. on leave.	
			1 O.R. reported from hospital	

2449 Wt. W14957/M90 750,000 1/16 J.B.C. & A. Forms/C.2118/12.

Army Form C. 2118.

Instructions regarding War Diaries and Intelligence Summaries are contained in F. S. Regs., Part II. and the Staff Manual respectively. Title Pages will be prepared in manuscript.

WAR DIARY
or
INTELLIGENCE SUMMARY
(Erase heading not required.)

Place	Date	Hour	Summary of Events and Information	Remarks and references to Appendices
BOIS GRENIER and RUE DU BOIS Sub-sectors	6.8.17		Numbers 2, 3 & 4 Sections in the line. Indirect fire carried out on CROSS ROADS WEZ MACQUART (I22 b 95 80); DISTILLERY ROAD (I22 c d - b); GRAND MAISNIL FARM (I33 d); CHATEAU D' HANCARDRY (I23 c 08). 1 O.R. admitted to hospital. The 2nd Battery Independent Machine Guns Heavy (2 B.I.M.P.) of the PORTUGUESE Expeditionary Force attached to this Coy for instruction left.	
	7.8.17		Numbers 2, 3 & 4 Sections in the trenches. Indirect fire carried out on LE GRAND MAISNIL FARM (I33 d); FLUER D'ECOSSE (I29 a 22); DISTILLERY ROAD (I22 b, c d b); ESTAMINET D'LA BARRIERE (I22 b 05). 1 O.R. proceeded to BOULOGNE to fetch a remount.	
	8.8.17		Numbers 2, 3 & 4 Sections in the trenches. Indirect fire carried out on LE GRAND MAISNIL FARM (I33 d); FLUER D'ECOSSE (I29 a 22); DISTILLERY ROAD (I22 b. c d & b); CROSS ROADS WEZ MACQUART (I22 b 95 80).	
	9.8.17		Numbers 2, 3 and 4 sections in the trenches. Indirect fire carried out on CROSS ROADS WEZ MACQUART (I22 b 95 80); DISTILLERY ROAD (I22 b c, d & b); ESTAMINET D'LA BARRIERE (I22 b 05); HALT MONT PINDO (I34 a); FLEUR D'ECOSSE (I29 a 22). 1 O.R. reported from Hospital. 1 O.R. returned from leave.	

2449 Wt. W14957/M90 750,000 1/16 J.B.C. & A. Forms/C.2118/12.

Instructions regarding War Diaries and Intelligence Summaries are contained in F. S. Regs., Part II. and the Staff Manual respectively. Title Pages will be prepared in manuscript.

WAR DIARY
or
INTELLIGENCE SUMMARY

(Erase heading not required.)

Army Form C. 2118.

Place	Date	Hour	Summary of Events and Information	Remarks and references to Appendices
BOIS GRENIER and RUE DU BOIS Sub-Sectors	10.8.17.		Nos 2, 3 + 4 Sections in the trenches.	
		7.45 PM	The enemy put down a heavy barrage in the RUE DU BOIS Sub-sector lasting half an hour. After a pause of 5 minutes an intense drum fire was opened which continued with more or less uniform volume for 1¼ hours. The sector between LEITH WALK and SALOP AVENUE being most severely dealt with both by T.Ms. and guns of all calibres up to 5.9s. Sometime during this bombardment a party of the enemy succeeded in penetrating within our lines as far as the first support line about I16a.55, as a Lebrety rifle and some stick grenades were subsequently found at this point. The enemy obtained no identifications. By 10-30 P.M. the situation was normal. Indirect fire carried out on FARM HOUSSAIN LE QUESNE, GRAND MAISNIL FARM, DISTILLERY, HOTTE HOUSSAIN FARM.	
	11.8.17		Nos 2, 3 + 4 Sections in the trenches. Indirect fire carried out on DISTILLERY ROAD (I22c d+b); ESTAMINET DE LA BARRIER (I22b05); BAS MAISNIL (N12a). 26 reinforcements arrived from 175 M.G. Coy. 1 other rank to U.K. on leave.	
	12.8.17.		Nos 2, 3 + 4 Sections in the trenches.	
		1-25 AM	The enemy put down a fairly heavy barrage on the front and support lines between CHARDS FARM (I16a) and WINE AVENUE (I16d). This barrage lasted for about 17 minutes but died down when retaliated upon by our artillery. Our machine guns cooperated by firing into the gaps between the front line and posts. Indirect fire carried out on DISTILLERY ROAD (I22c d+b) and ESTAMINET DE LA BARRIER (I22b05). 26 reinforcements reported from BASE. 1 Officer + 2 O.R. to 1st Army School of Instruction.	

2449 Wt. W14957/M90 750,000 1/16 J.B.C. & A. Forms/C.2118/12.

Instructions regarding War Diaries and Intelligence Summaries are contained in F. S. Regs., Part II. and the Staff Manual respectively. Title Pages will be prepared in manuscript.

WAR DIARY
or
INTELLIGENCE SUMMARY

(Erase heading not required.)

Army Form C. 2118.

Place	Date	Hour	Summary of Events and Information	Remarks and references to Appendices
BOIS GRENIER and RUE DU BOIS Sub-sectors	13.8.17		Nos 2, 3 + 4 Sections in the trenches. Indirect fire carried out on DISTILLERY ROAD (I 22 c d + b); and ESTAMINET DE LA BARRIER (I 22 b 05). 2 O.R. admitted to hospital. 1 O.R. from BOULOGNE with remount.	
	14.8.17		Nos 2, 3 + 4 Sections in the trenches. Indirect fire carried out on DISTILLERY ROAD (I 22 c d + b) and ESTAMINET DE LA BARRIER (I 22 b 05).	
	15.8.17		Nos 2, 3 + 4 Sections in the trenches. Indirect fire carried out on LA HOUSSOIE ~~FARM~~ HOTEL (I 27 c); ROAD (I 34 b 9. 8); DISTILLERY ROAD (I 22 c d + b); ESTAMINET DE LA BARRIER (I 22 b 05). 1 Officer returned from Rest Camp.	
	16.8.17		Nos 2, 3 + 4 Sections in the trenches. Machine Guns cooperated in bringing heavy fire to bear on INCOME SUPPORT and LA HOUSSOIE TRAMWAY, in order to drown the noise made by our Infantry in putting Bangalore torpedoes under enemy wire. The detonation gave good results. Indirect fire was carried out on DISTILLERY ROAD (I 22 c d + b); and ESTAMINET DE LA BARRIER (I 22 b 05).	
	17.8.17		Nos 2, 3 + 4 Sections in the trenches. Machine Guns again cooperated with artillery whilst Infantry were putting out Bangalore torpedoes. Indirect fire carried out on to DISTILLERY ROAD (I 22 c d + b); and ESTAMINET DE LA BARRIER (I 22 b 05). 1 Officer to U.K. on leave. 1 O.R. reported from BASE.	

2449 Wt. W14957/M90 750,000 1/16 J.B.C. & A. Forms/C.2118/12.

Army Form C. 2118.

Instructions regarding War Diaries and Intelligence Summaries are contained in F. S. Regs., Part II. and the Staff Manual respectively. Title Pages will be prepared in manuscript.

WAR DIARY
or
INTELLIGENCE SUMMARY
(Erase heading not required.)

Place	Date	Hour	Summary of Events and Information	Remarks and references to Appendices
BOIS GRENIER and RUE DU BOIS Subsection	18.8.17		Nos 2, 3 + 4 Sections in the line. Indirect fire carried out on to DISTILLERY ROAD (I22 c d+b); ESTAMINET DE LA BARRIER (I22 b 05); DUMP near ELBOW ROAD (I28 c); LA HOUSSOIE TRAMWAY (I27). 1 Officer returned from U.K. 1 O.R. admitted to Hospital (sick).	
	19.8.17		Nos 2, 3 + 4 Sections in the line. Indirect fire carried out on to FARM HOUSSAIN (O 2a); MOTTE HOUSSAIN FARM (I32 d); FORK ROADS S.E. of GRAND MAISNIL FARM (I33 c); in support of Infantry patrol inspecting gaps made in enemy wire by bangalore torpedoes. Indirect fire was also carried out on to LA HOUSSOIE TRAMWAY (I27); ROAD (I34 b 00.85); DISTILLERY ROAD (I22 c d+b); ESTAMINET DE LA BARRIER. 1 Officer to U.K. on leave. 1 O.R. for course to 1st Army Gas School. 3 O.R. reported from Anti-aircraft course.	
	20.8.17		Nos 2, 3 + 4 sections in the trenches. Indirect fire carried out on I27 c 00.14; I27 a 61.69; and O3 b 43.85 in support of Infantry patrol going out to examine enemy wire. Indirect fire was also carried out on to LA HOUSSOIE (I27); DUMP at ELBOW ROAD (I28 c); DISTILLERY ROAD (I22 c d+b); and ESTAMINET DE LA BARRIER (I22 b 05). 1 N.C.O. reinforcement from BASE. 1 O.R. wounded in ERQUINGHEM. The enemy fired 50 shells into ERQUINGHEM causing a few casualties.	

2449 Wt. W14957/M90 750,000 1/16 J.B.C. & A. Forms/C.2118/12.

Instructions regarding War Diaries and Intelligence Summaries are contained in F. S. Regs., Part II. and the Staff Manual respectively. Title Pages will be prepared in manuscript.

WAR DIARY
or
INTELLIGENCE SUMMARY
(Erase heading not required.)

Army Form C. 2118.

Place	Date	Hour	Summary of Events and Information	Remarks and references to Appendices
BOIS GRENIER and RUE DU BOIS Sub sectors	21.8.17.		Nos 2, 3 + 4 Sections in the trenches. Indirect fire carried out on to DUMP (I 27 c 1.1); THE GAP (O 2 d); ROAD near STATION - LA HOUSSOIE (I 27 b); ESTAMINET DE LA BARRIER (I 22 b 0 5); DISTILLERY ROAD (I 22 c d + b); THE HALT - MONT PINDO (I 34 a); GRAND MAISNIL FARM (I 33 c + d). Machine Guns also engaged hostile aircraft. 1 O.R. admitted to hospital (sick).	
	22.8.17		Nos 2 3 + 4 Sections in the trenches. Indirect fire carried out on to INCOME AVENUE (MOTTE HOUSSAIN FARM, (I 32 d), ROAD near STATION - LA HOUSSOIE (I 27 b), HALT - MONT PINDO (I 34 a), GRAND MAISNIL FARM (I 33 c + d), ESTAMINET DE LA BARRIERE (I 22 b 0.5), DISTILLERY ROAD (I 22 c d + b). 1.O.R admitted to hospital (sick).	
	23.8.17.		Nos 2, 3 + 4 Sections in the trenches. Indirect fire was carried out on to HALT - MONT PINDO (I 34 a), GRAND MAISNIL FARM (I 33 c + d). ESTAMINET DE LA BARRIERE (I 22 b 0 5), DUMP (I 27 c 1.1), MOTTE HOUSSAIN FARM (I 32 d). ROAD near LA HOUSSOIE STATION (I 27 b).	
	24.8.17.		Nos 2, 3 + 4 Sections in the trenches. Indirect fire carried out on to DUMP (I 27 c 1.1), MOTTE HOUSSAIN FARM (I 32 d), ESTAMINET DE LA BARRIERE (I 22 b 0.5), DISTILLERY ROAD (I 22 c. d + b), HALT - MONT PINDO (I 34 a), GRAND MAISNIL FARM (I 33 c + d).	
	25.8.17.		Nos 2, 3 + 4 Sections in the trenches. Indirect fire carried out on to ESTAMINET DE LA BARRIERE (I 22 b 0.5), DISTILLERY ROAD (I 22 c d + b), GRAND MAISNIL FARM (I 33 c + d), DUMP (I 27 c 1.1.), MOTTE HOUSSAIN FARM (I 32 d), LA HOUSSOIE (I 27). 2Lt Dyball wounded + admitted to hospital. C.Q.M.S. reported from 34th M.G. Coy. 1 O.R. to U.K. on leave.	

2449 Wt. W14957/M90 750,000 1/16 J.B.C. & A. Forms/C.2118/12.

Instructions regarding War Diaries and Intelligence Summaries are contained in F. S. Regs., Part II. and the Staff Manual respectively. Title pages will be prepared in manuscript.

WAR DIARY
or
~~INTELLIGENCE SUMMARY.~~
(Erase heading not required.)

Army Form C. 2118.

Place	Date	Hour	Summary of Events and Information	Remarks and references to Appendices
BOIS GRENIER and RUE DU BOIS Sub-sectors.	26.8.17		Nos 1, 3 + 4 Sections in the trenches No 1 section relieved No 2 section from LONDON BRIDGE Indirect fire carried out on to DUMP (I27c 1.1), ROAD near STATION - LA HOUSSOIE (I27b), GRAND MAISNIL FARM (I33c+d), ROAD at I34b 9.9), ESTAMINET DE LA BARRIERE (I22b 0.5), DISTILLERY ROAD (I22c d+b). 1 O.R. reported from course. 5 N.C.O's reported from BASE.	
	27.8.17		Nos 1, 3 + 4 Sections in the trenches. Indirect fire carried out on to DUMP (I27c 1.1), MOTTE HOUSSAIN FARM (I 32d), I31d.40.00, ESTAMINET DE LA BARRIERE (I22b 0 5), DISTILLERY ROAD (I22c d+b).	
	28.8.17		Nos 1, 3 + 4 Sections in the trenches. Indirect fire carried out on to MOTTE HOUSSAIN FARM (I32d), ESTAMINET DE LA BARRIERE (I22b 0 5), DISTILLERY ROAD (I22b c+d), ROAD at I34b 9.9. 4 signallers attached to this Coy from 2/5 Batt. S.L. Reg.	
	29.8.17		Nos 1, 3 + 4 Sections in the trenches. Indirect fire carried out on to MOTTE HOUSSAIN FARM (I32d), HALT MONT PINDO (I34a), ESTAMINET DE LA BARRIER (I22b 0 5), DISTILLERY ROAD (I22 bc+d), THE BREWERY (I22c 90.45), LARGE FARM (I22c). 1 Officer + 2 O.Rs left for A.A. course. 1 Officer + 1 N.C.O left for course at CAMIERES. Sgt Evans left for appointment as C.Q.M.S. to 20th M.G. Coy. 3 O.R. reported from BASE. L	

(A7092). Wt. W12839/M1293. 750,000. 1/17. D. D. & L., Ltd. Forms/C.2118/14.

Army Form C. 2118.

Instructions regarding War Diaries and Intelligence Summaries are contained in F. S. Regs., Part II. and the Staff Manual respectively. Title pages will be prepared in manuscript.

WAR DIARY
or
~~INTELLIGENCE SUMMARY.~~
(Erase heading not required.)

Place	Date	Hour	Summary of Events and Information	Remarks and references to Appendices
BOIS GRENIER and RUE DU BOIS Sub Sectors	30.8.17		Nos 1, 3 + 4 Sections in the trenches. Indirect fire carried out on to MOTTE HOUSSAIN FARM (I 32 d); HALT MONT PINDO (I 34 a) MINNIE EMPLACEMENT (I 27 b 70.15); THE BREWERY (I 22 c 90.45); LARGE FARM (I 22 c); ESTAMINET DE LA BARRIER (I 22 b 05); DISTILLERY ROAD (I 22 b c + d).	
	31.8.17		Nos 1, 3 + 4 Sections in the trenches Indirect fire carried out on to DUMP (I 27 c 1.1); I 33 a 62 95; NEW WORK (I 22 c 5.2) LA HOUSSOIE (I 27); ESTAMINET DE LA BARRIER (I 22 b 0.5); DISTILLERY ROAD (I 22 c d + b). 1 Officer reported from leave. 1 O.R. reported from hospital.	

C A White
Capt.
Commdg 172nd Tunl. Coy. R.E.

(A7092). Wt. W12839/M1293. 750,000. 1/17. D. D. & L., Ltd. Forms/C.2118/14.

Operation Order No 9 (Contd)

No 1

(4) Diversion

A side show will be made by Artillery, French Mortars, Flame Projectors, and all available Machine Guns on WEZ MACQUART and trenches in the vicinity. There will also be a smoke diversion opposite WEZ MACQUART and dummy figures will be manipulated in order to simulate an advance at this point.

) Machine Guns

At Zero – 3 minutes 13 guns will place a barrage on the area Incident Alley, Incident Drive, and Incident Row during the raid, as shown in Table Appendix I. The guns will be relieved at Zero – 4 hours by Lewis Guns, and will then proceed to their Battery Positions. S.A.A and water will be sent to Battery Positions from Coy. H.Q under arrangements made by 2nd i/c, and O.C Sections will have their Guns, Belt Boxes etc in position at Zero – 2 hours. Guns must be laid, and fitted with substantial depression stops (where guns are traversing with traversing stops) at Zero – 1½ hours ready for inspection by O.C. Coy.

(6) Rate of Fire.

From Zero – 3 minutes to Zero + 40 minutes, guns will fire at the rate of 80 to 100 rounds per minute. From Zero + 40 minutes to Zero + 65 minutes, at maximum rate of fire.

From Zero + 65 to Zero + 70 fire will gradually die down.

From Zero + 70 to Zero + 90 guns will remain in position ready to put down a further barrage if called for. At Zero + 90 Guns will return to usual positions.

7) Communication

"A" Battery will be connected by Telephone to H.Q of O.C. raiding Battalion. One runner from each Battery will be at No 4 Position (Top of Wellington Avenue) at Zero – one hour

) Reports.

To O.C. Company at Left Battalion Headquarters.

) Rocket Signal.

(A) In the event of O.C. raid firing a Blue Star Rocket, (which will be repeated at Battalion Headquarters) the Artillery will continue to fire as in Phase 4, for a further quarter of an hour.

(B) Should this Rocket be fired before Zero hour it will mean that the operation is postponed one hour

(C) In case B, confirmation by Telephone or Runner will be sent to O.C. Batteries

) Synchronization of Watches.

2nd i/c will see that all watches are synchronized at Zero – 4 hours

). Zero.

Will be notified later

2)

Acknowledge.

Issued at

by Runner.

Copy No 1.	172nd Brigade	Copy No 8	O.C No 4 Section
2.	O.C 2/4th S.L.R.	9	War Diary
3	O.C 171 M.G. Coy.	10	" "
4	D.M.G.O.	11	172nd L.T.M.B.
5	O.C No 1 Section	12	D.L.O.
6	O.C No 2 "	13)	Spare
7	O.C No 3 "	14)	

[signature]

SECRET Operation Orders No. Copy No.

By Lieut C. M. Howard In the Field 23-7-17

Commanding 172 M. G. Coy.

Ref. Map 36 N.W. 4 7th 1:10000

Special Map attached.

(1) Information. A series of minor offensive operations will be carried out by the 172nd Infantry Brigade with the following objects:-

(A) To deceive the enemy opposite us as to the strength in which we are holding our line and with regard to the real policy which the Brigade is adopting.

(B) To prevent him withdrawing any of his Troops or Artillery.

(C) To capture prisoners

(D) To secure Identification

(E) To capture material

(F) To inflict casualties

(G) To destroy dugouts and defences of the Area against which the operations are directed.

(2) Intention.

D Coy of the 2/4th Battalion S.L.R. will raid the enemy's lines.

The area to be raided is the Quadrilateral.

I 22 a 30.55

I 22 a 16.43.

I 22 a 30.32

I 22 a 46.42.

and the support line

I 22 a 40.43.

To I 22 a 50.43.

The raid in all further references will be called the "Fox Trot"

(3) General Outline. These operations will be divided into 4 phases commencing at Zero minus 3½ minutes.

1st Phase Zero minus 3½ minutes to Zero. Infantry will be in position about 100 yards from enemy trench ready to assault.

2nd Phase. Zero to Zero + 4 minutes. Barrage lifts and Infantry at once enter enemy front line trenches and the leading men push down the communication trenches towards support line

3rd Phase Zero + 4 minutes to Zero + 40 minutes. During this phase the raiding party are distributed all over the area to be raided.

4th Phase Zero + 40 minutes to Zero + 65. Infantry withdrawal commences. Artillery continue firing till Zero + 45 minutes.

Vol 8

Confidential

No: 172. MACHINE. GUN. Coy. WAR. DIARY.
September 1917.

SECRET   Copy No. 1.

Operation Order No 10
By Capt. G. A. Wade
Commdg 172nd M.G. Coy

Map Reference BOIS GRENIER 1:10,000
Sheets 36 - 36a 1:40,000
HAZEBROUCK 5a 1:100,000

15/9/17

1. The 172nd M.G. Coy will be relieved by the 113th M.G. Coy on the 17th September 1917.
2. On relief the 172nd M.G. Coy will move, with the 57th Division, into Army Reserve in the ST HILAIRE Area. The relief must be complete before dusk on the 17th Sept 1917.
3. Nos 1, 2 & 4 Sections will be relieved by Nos 1, 2 & 4 Sections of the 113th M.G. Coy which will leave Company H.Q. at 9.30 a.m with guns etc on handcarts which will bring back guns etc of this Company. O.C. No 3 Section will have 12 guides detailed to guide gun teams to each of the twelve gun positions mentioned in the attached Relief table.
4. Belt Boxes will be handed over to the 113th Machine Gun Company and a corresponding number received from them at Coy H.Q. after relief.
5. On the night of 16th/17th the following will be returned to Coy H.Q. by the Ration Limber :-
(1) All men's packs
(2) Spare Parts boxes (Spare Parts wallet only will be kept in the trenches)
(3) Trench [illegible]
(4) Periscopes
(5) Hyposcopes.
(6) Lamps etc
(7) Belt filling machines
(8) Light tripods
(9) Any [illegible] to send back.
(10) Axes, bill hooks, sickles
6. At 10 a.m each gun team will have neatly arranged in some convenient place about 5 yds from gun position the whole of its material ready for carrying away. The dug outs, emplacements must be very carefully searched to ensure that no gun parts, equipment etc has been left behind. At the same time the latrines will be emptied and everywhere thoroughly cleaned up. When the relieving team arrives their gun and material will be placed quite separate from the material mentioned above and the position handed over in the usual manner, all points concerning it will be brought to notice of relieving team, and following

[illegible] to be handed over to them:—

1. Emplacement book
2. Map showing S.O.S. target.
3. Any indirect fire particulars available
4. S.A.A. Water + Oil in battle positions
5. Reserve S.A.A. + Flares
6. Any other articles such as rattles, latrine buckets [illegible] attached to the positions
7. Trench mountings and disappearing mountings (if any)
8. A.A. mountings
9. Belt Boxes [illegible].

Receipts in duplicate will be obtained and a certificate (attached) to the effect that the position was handed over spotlessly clean and in order.

7. N.C.O's in charge of stopping guns must explain very thoroughly the limits of traverse and when fire is opened. The position of indirect fire positions battle positions + A.A. mountings must also be carefully pointed out.

8. When receipts + certificate have been obtained teams will proceed, carrying all their material to the handcarts, and return at once to Company HQ by routes indicated in Table. There must be at least 200x interval between hand carts.

9. Officers will hand over and obtain duplicate receipts for:—
   (1). A full account of the system their guns are worked on.— ration supply, water supply, S.A.A. supply. Any characteristics of their sector + positions
   (2) All trench maps, air photos, etc in possession.
   (3) All trench stores, Stocks of S.A.A. + Flares etc

10 ACKNOWLEDGE.

E.H.G. Mainwaring. Lt.
for O.C. 172 Machine Gun Coy.

Distribution — Issued through signals at p.m Sept 16th 1917.

No 1 } War Diary
" 2 }
" 3 O.C 113th M.G. Coy
" 4 Lt Mansergh
" 5 2/Lt Vyryan
" 6 2/Lt Greenwood
" 7 2/Lt Gadd
" 8 Lt McGrath
" 9 Transport Sergt.
" 10 C.S.M.
" 11 C.Q.M.S
" 12 Spare.

Appendix I.

Relief Table.

Section	Takes handcart as far as	And carries guns etc to relieve team at.	Officer will relieve:–	Remarks.
1 team 2 team 3 team 4 team } 1	1 { CROMBALOT DUMP by direct route 2 { Junction of SHAFTESBURY AV. and road through BOIS GRENIER	H 30 - 1 H 30 - 2 I 25 - 1 I 25 - 2	LT GREENWOOD at LONDON BRIDGE.	No 1 Section loads 2 guns on each of 2 handcarts.
1 team 2 team 3 team 4 team } 2	3 { FIRE STATION CHAPELLE D'ARMENTIERES I 9 c 3 8. 4 { Do.	I 14 I 15 - 2 I 15 - [illegible] I 9 - 1	Sergt. will relieve LT VIVYAN at LILLE POST	do. Via Emergency Road P RUE MARLE, CROWN PRINCE RD; LILLE RD.
1 team 2 team 3 team 4 team	5 { Puts off one gun at WINDYGATE Dump I 19 b 31 [illegible] RATION FARM 6 { RATION FARM	I. 21 I 20 - [illegible] I 20 - 2 I 20 - 3	LT McGRATH at dugout in SUBSIDIARY LINE left of PARK ROW.	do.

Certificate to be obtained from each relieving Gun Team.

This is to certify that No ...... Machine Gun Position was handed over to 113th M.G. Coy at .... on Oct 17th 1917 in thorough repair and spotless clean

Signed ....

Army Form C. 2118.

Instructions regarding War Diaries and Intelligence Summaries are contained in F. S. Regs., Part II. and the Staff Manual respectively. Title pages will be prepared in manuscript.

WAR DIARY

~~or~~

~~INTELLIGENCE SUMMARY.~~

(Erase heading not required.)

Place	Date	Hour	Summary of Events and Information	Remarks and references to Appendices
BOIS GRENIER and RUE DU BOIS			REF: TRENCH MAP. BOIS GRENIER – sheet 36 N.W.4. Edition 6D. Scale 1:10,000, and TRENCH MAP RADINGHEM sheet 36.S.W.2. Edition 6D Scale 1:10,000.	
	1.9.17.		Indirect fire carried out by night on Road at O2d17 to O2d.5.2; Road at I32c.02.13 to O2a 8.8. Road at O8b.7.9 to O8b.99.60; DISTILLERY ROAD. ESTAMINET DE LA BARRIERE. NEW WORKS & SCREEN I22C 5.2. LA HOUSSOIE I27a.6.3. 1.O.R. to U.K. on leave. Nos. 2 3 & 4 Sections in the trenches.	
	2.9.17		Indirect fire carried out on NEW WORKS & SCREEN I22c 5.31; LA HOUSSOIE O2d 1.7 to O2d.5.2. O8b.8.8 to O8b.99.60. 3.O.R rejoined from M.G.C Base Depot. Nos. 2. 3 & 4 Sections in the trenches.	
	3.9.17		Indirect fire carried out on O1a.90.75: I27c 80.80 to I27c 8.9: I22C 53.10: I27a.6.3. 1 O.R admitted to Hospital (Sick) Nos 2.3 & 4 Sections in the trenches	
	4.9.17		Indirect fire carried out on Road O1c.58 O7a.95; Road I33a 70.95 to I27c.9.8. NEW WORK at I22c.53.10 LA HOUSSOIE. No 1. Section relieved No 3 Section in the line.	
	5.9.17		Indirect fire carried out on NEW WORK I22C 53.10; LA HOUSSOIE; ROAD O1C.50.80 to O7a 90.50; Road I33a.60.95 to I27.C.80.70. Nos 1.2 & 4 Sections in the line. 2 O.R. proceeded on a Divisional Signalling Course.	
	6.9.17		Indirect fire carried out on NEW WORK I22C.53.10; Road O1c 5.8 to O7a 95; Road I33a 7.9 to I27c.9.8. I25.C.53.10. LA HOUSSOIE. Lt N.S.St.G. MANSERGH joined the Coy as 2nd in Command.	
				[signature] Capt Commdg 172nd Inf Coy

(A7092). Wt. W12839/M1293. 750,000. 1/17. D. D. & L., Ltd. Forms/C.2118/14.

Instructions regarding War Diaries and Intelligence Summaries are contained in F. S. Regs., Part II. and the Staff Manual respectively. Title pages will be prepared in manuscript.

WAR DIARY
or
~~INTELLIGENCE~~ SUMMARY.
(Erase heading not required.)

Army Form C. 2118.

Place	Date	Hour	Summary of Events and Information	Remarks and references to Appendices
	7/9/17		Indirect fire carried out on NEW WORKS and SCREEN I22 C 5.2. LA HOUSSOIE I27 A 6.3 O1A 4.0 O7A 95.55. I33A 65.95 – I27c 8.6 I22 c 53.10 I33 B 99.45 and NEW WORK at I22. C 53.10. 1 O.R. returned from leave	
	8/9/17		Indirect fire carried out on WEZ MACQUART I22 b 95.75 – TRACKS I23 c 9.3. NEW WORK I22 c 53.10. HALT MOND PINDO O1A 4.0 to O7A 95.55. I33A 65.95 to I27c 86 I22c 53.20. NEW WORK I22 c 5.2 LA HOUSSOIE I27 A. 6.3 INCLEMENT TRENCH I22. A.	
	9/9/17		Indirect fire carried out on LA GRANDE MAISNIL FME I33 d 05.20 BREWERY I22 c 90.45 MOTTE HOUSSAIN FME I32 d 05.60 NEW WORK at I22 c 53.10. Tracks at I23 c 9.3. X roads WEZ MACQUART I22 b 95.75 O1A 4 – O7a 95.55 – HALT MONT PINDO I33a 65.95. I27c 8.6 – I22 c 53.10. 2 O.R. to Army rest camp. 2 O.R. to hospital. 2nd Lt ACKROYD proceeded on leave to U.K. 10/9/17 – 20/9/17	
	10/9/17		Indirect fire carried out on TRACKS I23 c 9.3. X rds WEZ MACQUART I22 c 95.85. CHATEAU D'HANCARDY I29a 85.95 THE GAP O2 6 0.4 LA MOTTE HOUSSAIN FME I32 d 10.60. GRAND MAISNIL FME I33 D 05.20. BREWERY I22 c 90.45. MOTTE HOUSSAIN FME I32 d 05.60. 1 O.R. returned from Corps Rest Station.	
	11/9/17		Indirect fire carried out on LA GRANDE MAISNIL FME I33 d 05.20. BREWERY I22 c 90.45. MOTTE HOUSSAIN FME I32 d 2.6. GRAND MAISNIL FME I33 d 1.2. HALT MOND PINDO I34 a 0.2. CHATEAU D'HANCARDY I29a 85.95. TRACKS I27c 9.3. X roads WEZ MACQUART I22 b 97.85 The guns at LONDON BRIDGE I25 d. 3.9 opened fire from their S.O.S positions on a red light being sent up. All was quiet in a few minutes; the artillery did not fire.	E. Ll. [illegible] Capt. Commdg 172nd Inf Coy

(A7092). Wt. W12839/M1293. 750,000. 1/17. D. D. & L., Ltd. Forms/C.2118/14.

Instructions regarding War Diaries and Intelligence Summaries are contained in F. S. Regs., Part II. and the Staff Manual respectively. Title pages will be prepared in manuscript.

WAR DIARY
or
~~INTELLIGENCE~~ SUMMARY.
(Erase heading not required.)

Army Form C. 2118.

Place	Date	Hour	Summary of Events and Information	Remarks and references to Appendices
	12/9/17		Indirect fire carried out on CHATEAU D'HANCARDRY I29a 85.95. Tracks I23c 9.3. LE GRAND MAISNIL FME I33d 05.20. I32a 45.30. at the request of the C.O. [illegible] Batt: to assist ~~at~~ T.M. Barrage at 5.30. 2 hr. 2nd Lt Vyvyan and 3 O.R's returned from A.A. Course.	
	13/9/17		Indirect fire carried out on THE GAP O2 B.0.4. LAMOTTE HOUSSAIN FARM I32d 10.60. GRAND MAISNIL FARM I33d 1.2. I29a 85.95 CHATEAU D'HANDCARDRY. The BREWERY. I22c THE HALT. MONT PINOD. 1. O.R to Hospital. 1 O.R from leave in U.K	
	14/9/17		Indirect fire carried out on the GAP O2 B.0.4 LA MOTTE HOUSSAIN FARM I32d 1.6. GRAND MAISNIL FARM. I33d 1.2. I26d 05.10 to I26d 25.50 LA HOUSSOIE I29a 6.3.	
	15/9/17		Indirect fire carried out on CROSS Rds FLEUR d'ECOSSE I29a 05. 3. 1 O.R returned from leave in U.K. and 1 O.R went to Hospital.	
	16/9/17		An advance party of the 113th M.G. Coy arrived for making preparations for the relief. 2 O.R returned from Signalling Course.	
ESTAIRES	17/9/17		The Company was relieved by the 113th M.G. Coy and marched to ESTAIRES where they were billeted, the men in FONTAINE BUILDINGS. Officers in billets: REF. MAP. FRANCE. 36A	O.O 2013 [illegible]
	18/9/17		The Coy remained at ESTAIRES in billets.	
				[signature] Capt. Commdg 172nd [illegible] Coy

(A7092). Wt. W12839/M1293. 750,000. 1/17. D. D. & L., Ltd. Forms/C.2118/14.

Instructions regarding War Diaries and Intelligence Summaries are contained in F. S. Regs., Part II. and the Staff Manual respectively. Title pages will be prepared in manuscript.

WAR DIARY

~~or~~

~~INTELLIGENCE SUMMARY.~~

(Erase heading not required.)

Army Form C. 2118.

Place	Date	Hour	Summary of Events and Information	Remarks and references to Appendices
	19/9/17		REF. MAP FRANCE 36A 1:40.000 The Coy marched to LE HAMEL (V21 B 2.1) and LENGLET (V22.A.7.5) and billeted there for the night.	
	20/9/17		The Coy marched to PIPPEMONT (S.15 central) and were billeted in various farm houses.	
	21/9/17		An inspection by section Officers of kit and gun equipment took place in the morning 2nd Lt ACKROYD returned from, and 2nd Lt JONES went on, leave to the U.K. the latter as from the 22nd Sept 1.O.R. reformed from M.G.C Base Depot and 1.O.R. from hospital. 1 O.R. went to Hospital.	
	22/9/17		4 O.Rs relinquish to duty with their battalion (Signallers) ~~Inspection by the C.O~~	
	23/9/17		Church Parade at 5.15 p.m. – Two O.R went to Hospital sick. 2 O.R returned from Rest Camp.	
	24/9/17		Training commenced. The following programme was carried out. 8.15 a.m. Sections parade at billets under Section Officers. 8.30–9.30 a.m. Gun drill by sections. 9.45–10.45 a.m. Use of Compass – Officers. Drill – Men. 10.45–11.45 a.m. Instruction in Range finding, Scouting, Signalling, Lewis Gun etc in small classes. 11.45. 12.45 Lecture & demonstration Limber Packing – 12.45. 1 p.m. Limber Packing – 2.15. 3.15 p.m. Limber Packing – 3.15–4.15 p.m. Games & Backward Classes & Range. Two O.R to complete course in signalling – 1 O.R joined and was posted to No 4 Section –	
				[signature] Capt. Commdg 177th Coy

(A7092). Wt. W12839/M1293. 750,000. 1/17. D. D. & L., Ltd. Forms/C.2118/14.

Army Form C. 2118.

Instructions regarding War Diaries and Intelligence Summaries are contained in F. S. Regs., Part II. and the Staff Manual respectively. Title pages will be prepared in manuscript.

WAR DIARY

or

~~INTELLIGENCE SUMMARY.~~

(Erase heading not required.)

Place	Date	Hour	Summary of Events and Information	Remarks and references to Appendices
PIPPEMONT.	25/9/17.		Training Programme – 8.15 a.m. Sections parade at billets under section Officers. 8.30 – 9.30 a.m. Gun drill 9.45 – 10.45 a.m. use of range under officers. Drill under Sergt Instructor – men – 10.45 – 11.45 a.m. Instruction in various subjects in small classes. 11.45 – 12.45 p.m. Lecture in Packsaddlery. 2.15 – 3.15 p.m. Practice Packsaddlery – 3.15 – 4.15 Games & Backward classes & range. 1 O.R. struck off the strength and 1 O.R. to hospital sick. No 99974 Pte Llewellyn T awarded 7 days F.P. No 1 for stealing fruit	
	26/9/17		Training Programme – 8.15 a.m. Sections Parade at billets under section Officers and march to the Training Ground wearing Box Respirators – 8.30 – 9.30 a.m. Competitive Gun Drill 9.45 – 10.45 a.m. Use of Field Telephone. Officers under O/c. Drill under Sgt Instructor for men – 10.45 – 11.45 a.m. Instruction in German M. Gun I.A. Mechanism etc. by small classes. 11.45 – 12.45 p.m. Physical Training. 2.15 – 3.15 p.m. Gun drill wearing respirators – 1 O.R. evacuated.	
	27/9/17		Training Programme – 8.15 a.m. Sections Parade at billets under section Officers and march to the Training ground. 8.30 – 9.30 a.m. Inter-section Competition ACTION. Panorama drawing – officers. Drill men. 10.45 – 11.45 Instruction in Mechanism, M.G. Signals etc. by small classes. 1.0 p.m. Lecture on BAYONET FIGHTING. by Major Anderson, Instructor 1st Army. 1 O.R. taken on the strength. 2 O.R. to hospital sick. 2 O.R. to a course of Signalling at the Divisional School. A commencement was made with the Company Sports in the evening.	
	28/9/17.		Training Programme – 8.15 a.m. Sections parade at billets under section Officers and march to Training ground wearing Box Respirators. 8.30 – 9.30 a.m. Action from Limbers. 9.45 – 10.45 Reconnaissance. Officers. Drill men – 10.45 – 11.45 a.m. Instruction in various M.G. subjects by small classes. 11.45 – 12.45 Scouting lecture and demonstration. 2.15 – 3.15 p.m. Barrage drill. 4.15 – 5.15 p.m. Games and Backward classes & one section on the range. Company sports were continued in the evening.	
				E. M. [illegible] Capt. Comndg 172nd M.G. Coy

(A7092). Wt. W12839/M1293. 750,000. 1/17. D. D. & L., Ltd. Forms/C.2118/14.

Army Form C. 2118.

Instructions regarding War Diaries and Intelligence Summaries are contained in F. S. Regs., Part II. and the Staff Manual respectively. Title pages will be prepared in manuscript.

WAR DIARY
or
~~INTELLIGENCE SUMMARY.~~
(Erase heading not required.)

Place	Date	Hour	Summary of Events and Information	Remarks and references to Appendices
PIPPEMONT	29/9/17		Training Programme: Sections Parade at billets under Section Officers & march to Training grounds. 8.15 8.30-9.30am Inter Section Competition ACTION from limbers. 9.45-10.45am Use of Maps - Officers - Drill - men 10.45-11.45am Instruction in I.A. Mech: Range Cards Revolver drill by small classes. 11.45-12.45 Visual Training - 2.15-3.15 Barrage drill. 3.15-4.15 Games & Backward Classes & Range Work. 1 O.R to course of instruction - 1 O.R to leave in the U.K. - 2 O.R struck off the strength. Company & LT W G DONALDSON & 2 ORs returned from a Course of Instruction at CAMIERS	
	30/9/17		Training Programme Sections parade at billets under section officers and marched to Training ground at 9.15 a.m. 10-12 a.m. cleaning of guns equipment etc. In the afternoon the company sports were held. 1 O.R to hospital.	

[signature] Capt. Comdg 173rd Inf. Coy

(A7092). Wt. W12839/M1293. 750,000. 1/17. D. D. & L., Ltd. Forms/C.2118/14.

Instructions regarding War Diaries and Intelligence Summaries are contained in F. S. Regs., Part II. and the Staff Manual respectively. Title pages will be prepared in manuscript.

WAR DIARY
or
~~INTELLIGENCE~~ SUMMARY.
(*Erase heading not required.*)

Army Form C. 2118.

172 M G Coy
Vol 9

Place	Date	Hour	Summary of Events and Information	Remarks and references to Appendices
			REF: MAP THÉROUANNE	
PIPPEMONT. S15. central	1/10/17.		Training Programme – 8.30–9.30 am Action from Pack Saddles. 9.45–10.45 am Map making for Officers. Drill for men. 10.45–11.45 am Instruction in various subjects by small classes. 11.45–12.45 pm Lecture and Demonstration ATTACK use of ground & cover. 2.15–3.15 pm practice ATTACK. 3.15–4.15 pm Games & backward classes. 1 O.R. taken on the strength.	
	2/10/17		Training Programme. 8.30–9.30 am Inter-Section Competition Action from Pack Saddles. Company went to Baths until 2 pm. Officers – writing Operation orders – 3–4 pm Instruction in Range finding Sending M G Barrage etc by small classes. 11 O.R. transferred to 170 M G Coy. Auth: XI Corps A.78/34/6	
	3/10/17		Training Programme – 8.30–9.30 am Practice with auxiliary mountings. 9.45–10.45 am Use of Clinometer for Officers. Drill for men 10.45–11.45 am Instruction in M G signals. Barrage etc in small classes. 11.45–12.45 pm Lecture & Demonstration "Strong Points" – 2 O.2 Section on the Range. 8.30–12.30 pm. 1 O.R. evacuated to C.C.S. 2/Lt E.C. JONES returned from leave in the U.K.	
	4/10/17		Training Programme 8.30 Section [illegible] at [illegible] under Section Officers and [illegible] to Training Ground 8.40–9.30 am Attack [illegible] 9.45–10.45 am [illegible] Barrage Officers. Drill men 10.45–11.45 am Instruction in Range cards etc by small classes. 11.45–12.45 pm Lecture & Demonstration Advance [illegible] 8.30–12.30 pm [illegible] Section on the Range. 1 O.R. [illegible] C.R.S. – 5 O.R. [illegible]	

(A7092) Wt. W12839/M1293. 750,000. 1/17. D. D. & L., Ltd. Forms/C.2118/14

Instructions regarding War Diaries and Intelligence Summaries are contained in F. S. Regs., Part II. and the Staff Manual respectively. Title pages will be prepared in manuscript.

WAR DIARY
or
INTELLIGENCE SUMMARY.
(Erase heading not required.)

Army Form C. 2118.

Place	Date	Hour	Summary of Events and Information	Remarks and references to Appendices
[illegible] S.C./15 [illegible]	5/10/17		Training Programme. [illegible] Parade at billets under Section Officers [illegible] to Training Ground wearing Box Respirators. 8.20-9.30 am Trench to Trench attack. 9.45-[illegible] [illegible] [illegible] 10.45-11.45 am [illegible] [illegible] 8.30-[illegible] No 4 Section [illegible]	
	6/10/17		The Company was inspected as a Unit of the 172nd Inf Bde by the F.M.C.in.C. Sir Douglas Haig K.T. etc. 2nd Lt LE FIRMAND. S.G.b. 2Lt W.G. DONALDSON granted leave to the U.K. 6/10/17 – 16/10/17	
	7/10/17		Parades. 9.30 am Sections Parade at billets under Section Officers and march to Training ground for inspection by the C.O. 9.45 am. Inspection by C.O. Owing to the wet weather the Sports were postponed sine die. 1.O.R. returned from leave to the U.K. 1O.R. to Hospital sick.	
	8/10/17		Training Programme – 8.30 am. Parade at billets under Section Officers & march to training ground wearing Box Respirators. 8.40-9.30 am Indication & Recognition of Targets 9.45-10.45 Company Drill 10.45-11.45 am Barrage Training 11.45-12.45 pm Practice in Fire orders 12.45-1 pm Limber Packing	
	9/10/17		Training Programme :- 9.15 am. Parade at billets under Section Officers and march to training ground. Coy: Batting Parade 9.30 – 12.30 pm at FLECQUINELLE. NIGHT OPERATIONS Trench to Trench attack 12 pm – 10 am	
	10/10/17		Coy returned from NIGHT OPERATIONS at 10.30 am – Parade 2.45 p.m cleaning guns etc. 1.O.R evacuated sick – 4.O.R. returned from Signalling Course.	

(A7092). Wt. W12839/M1293 750,000. 1/17. D. D. & L., Ltd. Forms/C.2118/14.

Instructions regarding War Diaries and Intelligence Summaries are contained in F. S. Regs., Part II. and the Staff Manual respectively. Title pages will be prepared in manuscript.

WAR DIARY

~~or~~

~~INTELLIGENCE SUMMARY.~~

(Erase heading not required.)

Army Form C. 2118.

Place	Date	Hour	Summary of Events and Information	Remarks and references to Appendices
PIPPEMONT. MAP THEROUANNE S.15. central	11/10/17.		A Barrage Group was fired in co-operation with the other Machine Gun Coys of the division -	
	12/10/17.		Training Programme. 8.30. am Sections parade at billets under Section Officers & march to Training Ground wearing Box Respirators - 8.40 - 9.30. am Company Drill 9.45-10.45 Barrage Drill 10.45-11.45 Visual Training - 11.45 - 1.00 pm. Barrage Drill -	
	13/10/17.		Cleaning & Packing up in preparation for a move - 1.O.R. on leave to U.K. as from 14/10/17. 1. O.R. returned from leave in UK.	
	14/10/17.		Training Programme - 9.45 a.m Parade on Training ground with limbers packed ready for moving - move postponed for 3 days.	
	15/10/17.		Training Programme - 830-930 am - Company Drill - 9.45-10.45. am Barrage Drill - 10.45-11.45 am. Attack Practice using Pack Saddlery 11.45 - 1 pm Use of ground & cover - 8.30 am - 1 pm Range - attached men. 1OR to C.C.S.	
	16/10/17.		Training Programme - 830. am - 1 pm Practice attack on PIPPEMONT. including Barrages by Batteries moving forward etc: 8.30. am - 1 pm Range - attached men - 1.O.R to course of instruction at GRANTHAM.	
	17/10/17.		Training Programme - 8.30. am to 1 pm. Range - Inter-Section Competition to be fired in S. Box. Respirators - 1OR to Hospital - 2.O.R's evacuated to U.K.	
REF. MAP. HAZEBROUCK. 5A. BELGIUM 1:100,000	18/10/17.		The Coy marched to the RENESCURE area via. ESTREE. BLANCHE. and billeted in a farm house in the bend in the Road just below the V in RENESCORE.	

(A7092). Wt. W12839/M1293. 750,000. 1/17. D. D. & L., Ltd. Forms/C.2118/14.

Instructions regarding War Diaries and Intelligence Summaries are contained in F. S. Regs., Part II. and the Staff Manual respectively. Title pages will be prepared in manuscript.

WAR DIARY
or
~~INTELLIGENCE~~ SUMMARY.

(Erase heading not required.)

Army Form C. 2118.

Place	Date	Hour	Summary of Events and Information	Remarks and references to Appendices
	19/10/17		The Sections Embussed and moved to the PROVEN area via HAZEBROUCK - STEENVOORDE POPERINGHE billeting in tents and farm houses near the 20th Kilo on the PROVEN - POPERINGHE RD. The Transport marched to the same place via BAVINCHOVE - OXELAERE - WATOU - PROVEN 2nd Lt M.C. VYVYAN proceeded on leave to UK as from Oct 20th - Oct 30th	
	20/10/17		The company remained in billets cleaning up guns equipment etc	
	21/10/17		The company attended Church Parade at 9.30 a.m.	
	21/10/17		Training Programme. 9 a.m. cleaning of guns etc 10.11 gas box respirator drill. 1.O.R on leave 21st - 31 Oct	
	22/10/17		Training Programme 9 a.m Sections practicing carrying guns equipment etc 10.30 - 11.30 a.m Box respirator drill - 2.30 p.m Lecture by Section Officers "Machine Guns in attack" 2 O.R returned from leave in the UK. 1 O.R to hosp. sick	
	23/10/17		Training Programme 9 - 11.30 a.m Barrage drill - 2nd Lt Geddes and 13 O.Rs to XIV Corps Reinforcement Camp. 1 O.R. to hospital sick	
	24/10/17		Training Programme 9 a.m. cleaning up etc: In the afternoon the company moved to the PROVEN AREA No 1. MAP. BELGIUM & FRANCE. Sheet 27 - F.8.C 1 O.R evacuated -	

(A7092). Wt. W12839/M1295. 750,000. 1/17. D. D. & L., Ltd. Forms/C.2118/14.

Instructions regarding War Diaries and Intelligence Summaries are contained in F. S. Regs., Part II. and the Staff Manual respectively. Title pages will be prepared in manuscript.

WAR DIARY
or
~~INTELLIGENCE SUMMARY.~~

(Erase heading not required.)

Army Form C. 2118.

Place	Date	Hour	Summary of Events and Information	Remarks and references to Appendices
Sheet 28 BELGIUM & FRANCE F.& c.	25/10/17		Parade 9.30 am Cleaning of guns, equipment etc. Lt W G DONALDSON returned from leave having had an extension of 8 days owing to illness. 1. O R returned from Hospital 3. O R evacuated sick	
REF. MAPS Sheet 28 N.W. 1/20.000 Sheets 19. 20. 27. 28 1:40.000	26/10/17		Parade 9.30 am Cleaning of guns, equipment etc. On the night of the 26th 27th the Coy moved to the MALAKOFF area. The Transport marching and the personnel entraining to ELVERDINGHE thence marching to Solferino Camp. B 23 a 1.5 Sheet 28 1:40.000	
	27/10/17		Parade: 9.30 am cleaning of guns & equipment. 1 O.R. returned from leave in the U.K. 1. O.R proceeded on leave to U.K. 1 O.R proceeded to Corps Rest Station.	
	28/10/17		Parade 9 a.m Cleaning of guns & preparation for the trenches. Officers reconnoitred battle area beyond LANGEMARCK	
MAP BROEMBEEK 1:10.000	29/10/17		Parade 9 a.m. Cleaning of guns, camp etc and preparation for the trenches. 2 O.Rs to C.R.S. 2nd Lt ACKROYD & No 1 Section relieved 1 Section of 171 M.G Coy in the line H.Q. OLGA HOUSES V18 b 60/15	
	30/10/17		Parade 9 a.m. Cleaning of guns etc, oiling of feet in preparation for the trenches. 10-11 a.m Gun drill in Respirators. Officers, runners & NCOs reconnoitred line.	
	31/10/17		Parades 9.10 am Cleaning of guns etc. 10-11 am Gun drill in Respirators 11.12 am Emptying & Refilling of Belts. 12-12.30 oiling of Feet. 2nd Lt M.C Nyman returned from leave in the U.K. 1. O.R. to Hospital. Officers & NCOs reconnoitred line.	

(A7092). Wt. W12839/M1293. 750,000. 1/17. D. D. & L., Ltd. Forms/C.2118/14.

[signature] Commdg 172nd M.G. Coy Capt

Instructions regarding War Diaries and Intelligence Summaries are contained in F. S. Regs., Part II. and the Staff Manual respectively. Title pages will be prepared in manuscript.

WAR DIARY
or
~~INTELLIGENCE SUMMARY.~~
(Erase heading not required.)

Army Form C. 2118.

172 MG Coy
Vol 10

Place	Date	Hour	Summary of Events and Information	Remarks and references to Appendices
map: Belgium & France Sheet 28. 1:40.000.	1/11/17.		Parades 9. a.m. Cleaning of guns equipment etc. oiling of feet and treatment of Dg-feet. 2. O.Rs to Hospital —	
SCHAAP BALIE 1:10.000.	2/11/17		Parade - 9 a.m. Preparation for Trenches - The Coy relieved No 171 M.G.C on the 57th Divisional Front in the Evening 2/3rd Nov: (Appendix I). 1.O.R. wounded. 5. O.Rs Evacuated to C.C.S. Nos 3 & 4 Section went into the line - No 2 section remaining in reserve at SOLFERINO FM. Coy Hd Qrs at DROP HOUSE.	
	3/11/17		Parade. 9 a.m. Cleaning of guns. Sand bagging - oiling of feet. Comparatively quiet on the front until the night when S.O.S went up at 11.45. p.m. 12 belts per gun were fired from these at OLGA HOUSE. 52056 Cpl EASTWOOD. G.E was killed in Action. 1.O.R. wounded. Lt DONALDSON with No 2 Section relieved 2nd Lt ACKROYD with No 1 Section at OLGA HOUSES	
	4/11/17.		Parade - 9 a.m. Camp fatigues & oiling of feet - fairly quiet in the front line but back areas were heavily shelled from 4 pm until midnight - 5.30 a.m the guns at OLGA HOUSE combined with artillery in a barrage on the S.O.S lines.	
	5/11/17.		Parade. 9 am Camp fatigues & oiling of feet - Enemy artillery more active than usual on OLGA HOUSES & BOWER HOUSE. 1 O.R to Hospital sick. 3 O.Rs to C.R.S.	
	6/11/17.		Parade 9. a.m. Camp fatigues & oiling of feet. Guns at OLGA HOUSE put down a creeping barrage in combination with the Artillery - 2nd Lt ACKROYD with No 1 Section relieved 2nd Lt GREENWOOD with No 3 Section in the line. 3. O.R's wounded - 2 ORs to Hosp. sick and 2 O.R's to C.R.S.	

(A7092). Wt. W12839/M1293. 750,000. 1/17. D. D. & L., Ltd. Forms/C.2118/14.

To H. Q.
172 Inf. Bde.

172ND
MACHINE GUN
COMPANY.
No. 17/31/31.
Date. 30/11/17.

Herewith Original of War Diary for November 1917. please.

[signature] 2Lt.
for. O.C. 172 Machine Gun Coy.

[stamp] HEADQUARTERS
1-12-17
14W
INFANTRY BRIGADE

Instructions regarding War Diaries and Intelligence Summaries are contained in F. S. Regs., Part II. and the Staff Manual respectively. Title pages will be prepared in manuscript.

WAR DIARY

~~or~~

~~INTELLIGENCE SUMMARY.~~

(Erase heading not required.)

Army Form C. 2118.

Place	Date	Hour	Summary of Events and Information	Remarks and references to Appendices
7/	7/11/17		The Coy was relieved in the line by 6 guns of the 50 M.G. Coy. 6 guns of the 236 M.G. Coy. and returned to camp at SOLFERINO. Parade 9 a.m. Preparation for move. 1 O.R. on leave to U.K.	
MAP HAZEBROUCK 5A	8/11/17		The Coy less transport entrained at BOESINGHE for AUDRUICQ marching from there to BERTHAM to billets. The transport marched halting one night at LEDERZEELE.	
	9/11/17		Parade 9 a.m. cleaning of guns and equipment. No 31067 Sgt Smith H.W. proceeded to join his unit 2nd Gordon Highlanders having been given a commission. 2 O.R's to Hospital. Battle personnel returned from L.R. Camp.	
	10/11/17		Parade 9 a.m. cleaning of guns & equipment. Checking of kit etc. 1 O.R. from leave in U.K. 1 O.R. to hospital	
	11/11/17		Parade 9 a.m. inspection of kit & equipment. 1 O.R. returned from leave.	
	12/11/17		Parades 8.30 to 9 a.m. section drill, — 9-9.45 Classes — 9.45-10 Break — 10.30-12 Route march — 12-12.45 care & cleaning — 12.45-1.0 Ceremonial drill — 2.15-3.15 Officers & N.C.O's lecture "Discipline & Theory of fire", men care of feet. 4 O.R's to hospital.	
	13/11/17		Parades 8.30-9 Section drill — 9-9.45 Classes — 9.45-10 Break — 10.30-12.0 Tactical scheme 12-12.45 care & cleaning — 12.45-1 Ceremonial drill — 2.15-3.15 Officers & N.C.O's lecture map reading, theory of fire etc, men care of feet. 5 O.R's to C.C.S. 7 reinforcements from M.G. Base Depot	

(A7092). Wt. W12839/M1293. 750,000. 1/17. D. D. & L., Ltd. Forms/C.2118/14.

Instructions regarding War Diaries and Intelligence Summaries are contained in F. S. Regs., Part II. and the Staff Manual respectively. Title pages will be prepared in manuscript.

WAR DIARY

~~or~~

~~INTELLIGENCE SUMMARY.~~

(Erase heading not required.)

Army Form C. 2118.

Place	Date	Hour	Summary of Events and Information	Remarks and references to Appendices
MAP HAZEBROUCK 5A.	14/11/17		Parades 8-30-9-0 Section drill — 9-0-9-45 Classes — 9-45-10-0 Break — 10-0-12-0 Route march — 12-12-45 Care + cleaning — 2-0 Lecture on trench feet by A.D.M.S. 1 O.R. to hospital.	
	15/11/17		Parades 8-30-9-0 Section drill — 9-0-9-45 Classes — 9-45-10 Break — 10-0 Inspection of S.B.R. by Brigade Gas N.C.O. — 2-15 Officers + N.C.O's lecture "theory of fire" men care of feet. O.C. Coy to U.K. leave. Lt Mansergh assumes temporary command of Coy. 1 N.C.O. from hospital.	
	16/11/17		Parades 8-25 Coy parade for baths at NELLES. — 2-15 Care of feet — 3-30 Officers + N.C.O's lecture "map reading". 2 O.R's to course of signalling. 2 O.R's to hospital — 4 O.R's to C.C.S.	
	17/11/17		Coy parade for divine service. 2nd Lt BARBER leave to U.K. 1 N.C.O. to hospital. Coy canteen opened.	
	18/11/17		Parades 8-30-9-0 Section drill — 9-0-9-45 Classes — 9-45-10-0 Break — 10-45-12-15 Practice "Advance Guard" — 12-15-1-0 Care + cleaning — 2-15 Care of feet — 2-30 Lecture to Officers + N.C.O's on "Reconnaissance". 2 N.C.O's to course of instruction — anti-gas. 1 O.R. to hospital.	
	19/11/17		Parades 8-30-9-0 Section drill — 9-0-9-45 Classes — 9-45-10-0 Break — 10-0-10-45 Coy + Ceremonial drill — 10-45-12-15 Practice "Occupation of positions" — 12-15-1-0 Care + cleaning — 2-15 Care of feet — 2-30 Lecture to officers + N.C.O's "march discipline". No 1 Section on miniature range. Signallers: 8-30 to 11-30 Flag drill, Fullerphone practice, Shutter reading, Buzzer practice + lamp reading 6-0 to 7-0 P.M. 1 O.R. from hospital — 2 O.R. to hospital. 1 N.C.O. to U.K. for special course of instruction	

(A7092). Wt. W12839/M1293. 750,000. 1/17. D. D. & L., Ltd. Forms/C.2118/14.

Instructions regarding War Diaries and Intelligence Summaries are contained in F. S. Regs., Part II. and the Staff Manual respectively. Title pages will be prepared in manuscript.

WAR DIARY

~~or~~

~~INTELLIGENCE SUMMARY.~~

(Erase heading not required.)

Army Form C. 2118.

Place	Date	Hour	Summary of Events and Information	Remarks and references to Appendices
MAP HAZEBROUCK 5A.	20/11/17		Parades: 8-30-9-0 Section drill – 9-0-9-45 Classes – 9-45-10-0 Break – 10-0-10-45 Coy + ceremonial drill – 10-45-12-15 Tactical scheme "Attack" – 12-15-1-0 Care + cleaning – 2-15 Care of feet 2-30 Lecture to officers + N.C.O's "Use of compass". No 2 Section on miniature range. Signallers: from 8-30 to 12-45. Shutter reading (wearing S.B.R.) Lamp reading, Break, Station work shutter, Buzzer practice. 1 O.R. to hospital.	
	21/11/17		Parades: 8-30-9-0 Section drill saluting – 9-0-9-45 Classes – 9-45-10-0 Break – 10-10-45 Coy + ceremonial drill – 10-45-12-15 Tactical scheme "Ambushing a convoy" – 12-15-1-0 Care + cleaning, 2-15 Care of feet – 2-30 Lecture to officers + N.C.O's "M.G. Barrage". No 3 Section on miniature range. Signallers: from 8-30 to 12-45 Lamp reading + sending wearing S.B.R, Flag reading + sending, Break, Fullerphone practice, Map reading, setting with + without a compass, 6-0-7-0 PM Lamp reading. 2 N.C.O's from anti-gas course. 1 O.R. to U.K. on leave. 1 N.C.O + 1 O.R. to hospital.	
	22/11/17		Parades: 8-30-9-0 Section drill – 9-0-9-45 Barrage drill – 9-45-10-0 Break – 10-0-10-45 Ceremonial + Coy drill – 10-45-12-15 Tactical Scheme "Defence of a Village" – 12-15-1-0 Care + cleaning – 2-15 Care of feet – 2-30 Lecture to Officers + N.C.O's "Camouflage". No 4 Section on Miniature range. Signallers: from 8-30 to 12-45 Flag drill, Section work (flag), Break, Station work (shutter) Buzzer practice. Coy inspection + Transport by O.C. Lt P. McGrath to hospital.	

(A7092). Wt. W12839/M1293. 750,000. 1/17. D. D. & L., Ltd. Forms/C.2118/14.

Army Form C. 2118.

Instructions regarding War Diaries and Intelligence Summaries are contained in F. S. Regs., Part II. and the Staff Manual respectively. Title pages will be prepared in manuscript.

WAR DIARY

~~or~~

~~INTELLIGENCE SUMMARY.~~

(Erase heading not required.)

Place	Date	Hour	Summary of Events and Information	Remarks and references to Appendices
MAP HAZEBROUCK 5A	24/11/17		Parades: Coy parade for baths & pay. 1 O.R. to hospital. 1 O.R. to U.K. on leave.	
	25/11/17		Coy parade for Divine service. 1 O.R. to hospital – 1 N.C.O. from C.C.S.	
	26/11/17		Coy on large range at GUERMY 3A 2.7.	
	27/11/17		Inspection by G.O.C. 57' Division 1 O.R. to hospital. 1 O.R. evacuated.	
	28/11/17		4 sections attached to Battalions for Tactical Scheme under command of Battalion Commanders. Signallers: Flag drill, Pair reading & sending, lamp reading & sending, fullerphone. 1 OR from hospital.	
	29/11/17		Parades: 8.30-9.0 Section drill, N.C.O's communication drill, 9-0-9.45 Classes, 9.45-10.0 Break, 10.0-10.45 P.T., 10.45-12.15 Tactical scheme, 12.15-1.0 Care & cleaning, 2.0 Care of feet, 2.15 lecture by C.S.M. to Sect Sergts on "Pay parade" 2-30 No 3 Sect on range for rifle practice. No 4 Section on miniature range during morning. Signallers: Buzzer practice wearing S.B.R., Flag drill, Shutter reading, Buzzer practice, lamp reading. 1 O.R. on leave, 1 O.R. from leave, 1 O.R. from hospital, 2 O.R. to hospital.	

(A7092). Wt. W12839/M1293. 750,000. 1/17. D. D. & L., Ltd. Forms/C.2118/14.

Instructions regarding War Diaries and Intelligence Summaries are contained in F. S. Regs., Part II. and the Staff Manual respectively. Title pages will be prepared in manuscript.

WAR DIARY

~~INTELLIGENCE SUMMARY.~~

(Erase heading not required.)

Army Form C. 2118.

Place	Date	Hour	Summary of Events and Information	Remarks and references to Appendices
HAZEBROUCK 5A. 2A40.01.	30/11/17.		Parades: 8·30 Coy parade for Baths. 11-0 half of Coy parade for inoculation. 2·30 No 4 Section on range – rifle practice.	

[illegible] Lt.

O.C. 172 Machine Gun Coy.

(A7092). Wt. W12839/M1293. 750,000. 1/17. D. D. & L., Ltd. Forms/C.2118/14.

172nd Inf. Bde. [illegible]
CMGO [illegible]
O.C. 171st M. G. Coy. [illegible]
[illegible]
[illegible]
[illegible]

SECRET

[illegible]
[illegible]

War Diary

1. The 172nd Machine Gun Company will relieve the 171st Machine Gun Company in the 57th Divisional front on evening of 2/3 [illegible] 1917.
2. The guns will be [illegible] after relief as follows:-

Section	Section H.Q.	No. of Guns	Position of guns
1.	OLGA HOUSES	4	OLGA HOUSES ([illegible])
2.	SOLFERINO CAMP	4	SOLFERINO CAMP ([illegible])
3.	BESACE FARM.	1	REQUETE FARM.
3.		1	BESACE FARM.
3.		1	BOWER HOUSE.
3.	..	1	CONTROLING [illegible]
4.	OLGA HOUSES.	1	GRAVEL [illegible]
4.	..	1	SENEGAL FARM.
4.	..	2	OLGA HOUSES ([illegible])

3. The distribution of Battalions will be:-

2/4th [illegible] LINE.
2/10th [illegible] EAGLE TRENCH.
2/4th [illegible] MARSOUIN CAMP.
2/5th [illegible] HUDDLESTON CAMP.

4. The Company, less No. 2 Section, will move to DROP HOUSE [illegible] [illegible] at 4:30 p.m. 2/11/17. Each section will take the following equipment:-

Guns of No. 1 Section & [illegible] guns of No. 4 Section.
Gun ([illegible] waterproof sheet [illegible] [illegible])
Tripod
1st Aid Case (containing 1 [illegible])
Spare Barrel.
[illegible] rod.
4x2 oil
[illegible]
[illegible]
[illegible] 14 (8 taken forward 6 left at DROP HOUSE)
[illegible]
[illegible]
[illegible]

[illegible] of No. 4 [illegible]
[illegible] ([illegible] waterproof sheet [illegible])
[illegible]
1st Aid Case.
Spare Barrel.
4x2.
[illegible]
[illegible]
[illegible]
[illegible]
[illegible]
[illegible]
[illegible]
[illegible]
[illegible] 14 ([illegible] at DROP HOUSE & fetched later)

5. Men will carry [illegible] days Rations with them [illegible] [illegible] of the day's ration. [illegible] will be supplied from DROP HOUSE [illegible] [illegible] at present.

6. The arrangements [illegible] with O.C. 171st M. G. Coy. [illegible] will meet the [illegible] at DROP HOUSE at 4:30 p.m. guides for following:
one for REQUETE Fm. for 1 gun No. 3 Sect.
one for BESACE Fm. for [illegible] guns No. 3 Section.
one for CONTROLING Fm. for 1 gun No. 3 Sect.
[illegible] for OLGA HOUSES for [illegible] guns No. 4 [illegible].
[illegible] for BOWER HOUSE [illegible] No. 3 Section will [illegible] BESACE Fm.
Guides for GRAVEL FARM [illegible] SENEGAL Fm.
[illegible] No. 4 Section will be met at OLGA [illegible]
7. Every endeavour should be made to [illegible] [illegible] positions [illegible] [illegible]

[illegible]

[illegible] will be reported [illegible] giving the following information [illegible]

	10 a.m. DROP HOUSE [illegible]		NIL Return wanted:
	[illegible]	[illegible]	No.
	10.15 [illegible]	do.	No.
	[illegible]	[illegible] Casualty Return	YES
	[illegible]	[illegible]	—
	[illegible]	[illegible] Report	—

10. [illegible] Report [illegible] 2/7/17 [illegible] showing how the work [illegible]

11. As soon as guns are in position each Section officer will send back two runners (one to remain at Coy HQ and one to return with any messages from Coy HQ (DROP HOUSE).
Thoroughly reliable & intelligent runners only must be sent.

12. When EAST of [illegible] 800' [illegible] DROP HOUSE, [illegible] as possible [illegible] before [illegible] DROP HOUSE [illegible]

13. [illegible] DROP HOUSE [illegible] on night 31st/1st [illegible]

14. Men who are detailed to stay at [illegible] during the attack will accompany their Sections into the line.

15. The greatest care must be taken to avoid giving the gun position away by unnecessary movement or by smoke, [illegible]

16. Each Battery [illegible] will arrange for its own protection against [illegible] fire.

17. Each section will take [illegible] bottles of water. [illegible] will be [illegible] all the [illegible] orders. [illegible] that all [illegible] including officers, have been [illegible] will be [illegible] by Section Officer.

18. The guns which are at present at OLGA HOUSE putting down S.O.S. Barrage will have definite positions assigned to them to which they will move and form a [illegible] through our front line.

19. O.C. No. 4 Section will have 2 AA Sights, one at SENEGAL FARM and one at OLGA HOUSES. O.C. No. 3 Section will have an AA Sight on gun at COMPROMIS FARM.
ALL GUNS will fire at ALL hostile aeroplanes with exception of No. 1 Section's Battery.

20. ACKNOWLEDGE.

[illegible]
Capt.
Commanding 172nd [illegible]

[illegible]/7/17.

142 M.G.Coy.
Original
Vol 11

Instructions regarding War Diaries and Intelligence Summaries are contained in F. S. Regs., Part II. and the Staff Manual respectively. Title pages will be prepared in manuscript.

WAR DIARY
or
~~INTELLIGENCE SUMMARY.~~
(Erase heading not required.)

Army Form C. 2118.

Place	Date	Hour	Summary of Events and Information	Remarks and references to Appendices
BERTHEM	1.12.17		Nos 3 + 4 Sections took part in Tactical Schemes carried out by 2/5 Bn S L R + 2/9th Bn K L R on the RECQUES West Training Area.	
			1 O.R. to Leave (U.K.); 1 OR to Hospital (Sick).	
	2.12.17		Divine Services were held at 11.30 a.m. at NIELLES (C. of E.), at 9.30 a.m. at NIELLES for Nonconformists; and at 9.30 a.m. at NIELLES for Roman Catholics.	
			Nos 3 + 4 Sections were inoculated	
			Lt H.S. St G. MANSERGH relinquished temporary command of the Company on CAPT GAWADE returning from leave. 1 O.R. admitted to Military Hospital U.K.; 1 OR from Hospital	
	3.12.17		Training programme carried out	
			~~1 OR struck off the strength~~	
	4.12.17		The Company paraded for Baths at 8.25 a.m. A Commanding Officers inspection was held at 2.30 p.m.	
			1 Officer to Leave (Paris), 1 OR to Hospital; 1 OR from Hospital.	
			2/Lt H.A. Ockeshott joined the company from M.G.C. Base Depot.	
	5.12.17		The Company took part in a Brigade Tactical Scheme on the RECQUES Training Area.	
			2 Lt E.W. BARBER returned from Leave (U.K.); 2 OR returned from Courses; 1 O.R. to Course of instruction	
	6.12.17		Officers + N.C.O.s attended Lectures + demonstrations given by the Commandant XVIII Corps School at NORDAUSQUES.	
			The Transport moved from BERTHEM via NORDAUSQUES, BAVENGHEM, LEZ EPERLECQUE, GANSPETTE, WATOU to LEDERZEELE	
HERZEELE	7.12.17		The Transport resumed its trek passing through DROGEELE, RUBROUCK, WORMHOUDT to HERZEELE.	
			The Company entrained at AUDRUICQ Station at 5.55 am, detrained at PROVEN and marched	

E.N.S.E. Deane Capt

(A7092). Wt. W12839/M1293. 750,000. 1/17. D. D. & L., Ltd. Forms/C.2118/14.

Instructions regarding War Diaries and Intelligence Summaries are contained in F. S. Regs., Part II. and the Staff Manual respectively. Title pages will be prepared in manuscript.

WAR DIARY
or
~~INTELLIGENCE SUMMARY.~~
(Erase heading not required.)

172 M G Cy
Original

Army Form C. 2118.

Place	Date	Hour	Summary of Events and Information	Remarks and references to Appendices
	7.12.17		to HERZEELE	
			Lt W.G. DONALDSON assumed Temporary command of the Company during the absence of CAPT GAWADE caused by him taking over temporarily the duties of D.M.G.O.	
HERZEELE	8.12.17		The Company paraded for cleaning limbers, guns, equipment etc.	
			CAPT H S St G MANSERGH returned from leave and assumed command of the Company	
			1 OR to Leave (UK)	
	9.12.17		The Company paraded for Divine Services during the morning and for Baths during the afternoon.	
	10.12.17		The Company paraded for training in Gas precautions, Gun work etc	
	11.12.17		Training in Machine Gunnery was carried out during the day.	
	12.12.17	2.30 pm	The Brigadier General cmdg 172nd Inf Bde inspected the Company on Parade.	
			1 O.R from Hospital, 2 O.R from Leave (UK).	
	13.12.17		The Company paraded for Training	
	14.12.17		Training in Machine Gunnery was proceeded with.	
			1 OR to Leave (UK)	
	15.12.17		The Company paraded for a Route March at 9 a.m.	
	16.12.17		The day was spent in preparing for a move, cleaning & packing of limbers etc.	
ELVERDINGHE	17.12.17		The Company entrained at HERZEELE at 8.30 a.m. and proceeded by train via PROVEN to ELVERDINGHE. The Transport proceeded by road.	
			1 OR from Leave (UK)	
			Capt E. NEEDHAM assumed temporary command of the Company on Capt H.S. St G MANSERGH taking over command of 173 M G Cy	

E Needham Capt

(A7092). Wt. W12839/M1293. 750,000. 1/17. D. D. & L., Ltd. Forms/C.2118/14.

Instructions regarding War Diaries and Intelligence Summaries are contained in F. S. Regs., Part II. and the Staff Manual respectively. Title pages will be prepared in manuscript.

WAR DIARY
or
INTELLIGENCE SUMMARY.
(Erase heading not required.)

142 M.G. Coy
Original

Army Form C. 2118.

Place	Date	Hour	Summary of Events and Information	Remarks and references to Appendices
ELVERDINGHE	17.12.17		The Company relieved the 53rd M.G. Coy at MARGUERITE CAMP and took up the duties of M.G. Coy in Support.	
	18.12.17		The Company paraded at 9 a.m. for cleaning of guns, limbers, equipment etc & inspection of Respirators. 1 O.R. reported from M.G.C. Base Depot.	
	19.12.17		The Company paraded for training from 9 a.m. – 3 pm. ~~6 O.R. transferred~~ 1 O.R. from leave U.K.	
	20.12.17		The Company paraded for training from 9 a.m – 3 pm. 6 O.R. transferred to 143 M.G. Coy	
	21.12.17		The Company paraded for training from 9 a.m – 3 p.m.	
	22.12.17		The Company paraded for training from 9 a.m – 12.30 pm. All Officers & NCOs attended a lecture by the 57th Div. Intelligence officer on the subject of "Aeroplane Photographs Reports etc" at 2.30 pm.	
	23.12.17		The Company paraded for Divine Services. 1 Officer on leave to U.K.	
SIGNAL FARM U21c 1505.	24.12.17		The Company relieved 141 M.G. Coy & 170 M.G. Coy in the line. Headquarters were established at SIGNAL FARM (Sheet 20 S.W.4 U21 c 1505).	142 M.G. Coy O.O. A.
	~~25.12.17~~		~~2 O.R. to Hospital (Sick)~~. The following machine gun positions were occupied: Ref Sheets 20 S W 4. — U12 d 6384, U12 b 9020, U12 b 2595, U6 d 1812 and U12 b 2095 commanded by Lt DONALDSON G.; U6 c 9047, U6 c 8050, U5 d 5328 (2 guns) U5 d 4038 and U5 d 9525 commanded by 2/Lt VYVYAN. M.C.: U11 d 37 (2 guns)	

[illegible] Capt

(A7092). Wt. W12839/M1293. 750,000. 1/17. D. D. & L., Ltd. Forms/C.2118/14.

Instructions regarding War Diaries and Intelligence Summaries are contained in F. S. Regs., Part II. and the Staff Manual respectively. Title pages will be prepared in manuscript.

WAR DIARY
or
INTELLIGENCE SUMMARY.
(Erase heading not required.)

142 M G Coy
Original

Army Form C. 2118.

Place	Date	Hour	Summary of Events and Information	Remarks and references to Appendices
			and U12c 63 commanded by LT ACKROYD L.F.M.	
HOUTHULST FOREST SECTOR.	24.12.17.		LT DONALDSON + 2 LT VYVYAN had their headquarters at EGYPT HOUSE (U12b2095 Sheet 20SW4) and 2/LT ACKROYD'S headquarters were at PASCAL FARM (U12c 52 Sheet 20 SW4).	
	25.12.17		2 O.R. to hospital.	
	26.12.17		Guns fired at Enemy aircraft during the day. Carried out indirect fire on enemy roads and tracks during the night.	
		8pm	Opened fire on S.O.S. lines in response to signal on our right.	
			1 O.R from leave (UK).	
	27.12.17		1 OR to Hospital 1 OR wounded in action but remained at duty.	
	28.12.17		Intercompany relief. 2/LT JONES relieved LT DONALDSON at EGYPT HOUSE. Indirect fire was carried out by night on enemy tracks at U6b9910 (Sheet 20SW4) + on enemy positions V2c4015 (Sheet 20 SE 3) and P31d 5040 (Sheet 20 SE 3).	
	29.12.17	5.15pm	A barrage was put down on our Outpost line and Main defensive line. This was followed by a determined raid by a party between 40 and 50 strong on V1 to 2 Post. One of our machine guns fired on his S.O.S. lines in response to the signal from the Infantry. The raid was entirely repelled leaving the raid leader dead in our hands.	
			Indirect fire was carried out by night on enemy posts at V2c4015 + P31d 5040 (Sheet 20 SE 3.	

E N Sedham Capt

(A7092). Wt. W12839/M1293. 750,000. 1/17. D. D. & L., Ltd. Forms/C.2118/14.

Instructions regarding War Diaries and Intelligence Summaries are contained in F. S. Regs., Part II. and the Staff Manual respectively. Title pages will be prepared in manuscript.

WAR DIARY
or
INTELLIGENCE SUMMARY.
(Erase heading not required.)

Army Form C. 2118.

M2 MG Coy
Original

Place	Date	Hour	Summary of Events and Information	Remarks and references to Appendices
HOUTHULST FOREST SECTOR	30.12.17	8pm	Two companies of the 2/5th S. Lancs Regt attacked an enemy post at TURENNE CROSSING V1d (Sheet 20 SE 3.) Machine guns co-operated as per Operation Orders B. The 1st objective was taken and our line on the right was advanced about 200 yds. Our approximate new line ran in front of TURENNE CROSSING and V1c 7560 V1c 7510 + V7b 0080 (Sheet 20 SE). One prisoner was taken.	O.O.B.
			C.S.M. to leave (UK).	
	31.12.17		An officer of 55th Machine Gun Company reported at SIGNAL FARM to arrange details of relief.	
			Operation Order C issued	O.O.C.

E N [illegible] Capt

SW

Copy No. 1.

172 M. G. Coy.

OPERATION ORDER. No. 1

1. On the 24th Decr 1917 the 172nd M.G. Coy will relieve the 171st M.G. Coy & 170 M.G. Coy in the line.

2. Sections will go into the line with one N.C.O. to every two gun teams which will not consist of more than four men each.

3. Sections will consist of the following number of teams:–

No 1 Section	4 teams	
No 2 "	4 teams	
No 3 "	6 teams	
No 4 "	will remain in back area till called up.	

4. No 1 Section will relieve guns of 170 Coy. at PASCHL FARM & VEE BEND.
No 2 Section guns of 171 Coy. on the Railway and at EGYPT HOUSE.
No 3 Section the guns of 171 Coy at 5 Chemins, Pit Houses and FAIDHERBE Cross Roads.

5. No 1 Section will leave Coy H.Q. at 12 noon. Nos 2 & 3 Sections & H.Q. at 1 p.m.

6. Transport Officer will provide one half limber per Section except No 2 Section which will be one limber. H.Q. will utilise this with No 2 Section. Limbers will start with their respective Sections and will proceed as near to Signal Farm as possible.

7. Guides will be at SIGNAL FARM at 2 p.m. for No 1 Section and at 3 p.m. for Nos 2 & 3 Sections.

8. Battle order will be worn, one greatcoat and one blanket carried bandolier fashion rolled inside waterproof sheet. The unexpended portion of the days ration and two full days rations will be carried. Waterbottles will be full.

9. Relief complete will be reported to Coy H.Q. at SIGNAL FARM by runner from each Section.

10. 2/Lieut. Jones will move all details remaining in back area to LARRY CAMP and hand over [illegible] CAMP to 171 M.G. Coy.

11. Tripods & belt boxes will be taken over by Section Officers and receipt given to outgoing Section.

[signature illegible]
Capt.
Comdg 172 M.G. Coy.

Issued at 8:30 p.m.
23 · XII · 17.

Copy No 1 War Diary
No 2 171 M.G. Coy
3 172 Bde
4-7 S.O. (4)
8 T.O.
9. 170 M.G. Coy
10. Spare

SECRET

Copy No. ....

OPERATION ORDER B.
by O.C. PATTER.

1. At an hour to be notified later the Infantry will attack and consolidate an enemy post on our front.

2. This unit will assist by furnishing a barrage as below.

3. All preparations will be completed by 6 a.m. 30th inst.

4. O.C. M.Gs at PASCAL FARM & VEE BEND will have 10 belt boxes & 10 S.A.A. boxes per gun and the other Section Officers will have at least 8 belt boxes and 8 S.A.A. boxes at each gun. The best possible arrangements will be made for belt filling and this will be proceeded with as quickly as possible throughout the barrage.

5. ½ Lieut. Hyrgam will move his No 8 gun to a position 5 to 10 yards South of No 7 gun so that the pill box screens both guns from the North Side. Every gun utilised for this operation will be provided with flash screens.

6. ½ Lieut. Jones will instruct No 1 gun that they will only fire if they actually see the enemy advancing towards them and not as before instructed. Orders will be given in writing to N.C.O. i/c and a copy to be handed from sentry to sentry.

7. The barrage will last from Zero to Zero + 60 and guns will remain in position ready to open fire in case of counter attack till Zero + 180.
After this they will take up their ordinary S.O.S. lines.

8. The rate of fire throughout from Zero to Zero + 60 will be at the rate of 50 rounds per minute and S.O's will pay particular attention to fire control.

9. The guns will be laid and fired as shown in the following table:-

No of gun.	Map Reference	Direction (grid bearings)	Traverse.		Range	Elevation.
2.	U 12 d 63 87	30°	2°	Each way	1500^x	2° 35'
3.	U 12 b 25 95	96°	2°	" "	1800^x	3° 45'
7.	U 6 c 00 36	80°	6°	" "	2000^x	4° 48'
8.	U 6 c 00 24	80°	6°	" "	2100^x	5° 22'
9.	U 5 d 40 38	79°	3°	" "	2000 to 2300^x	4° 50' to 6° 40'
10.	U 11 b 70 60	80°	6°	" "	2300^x	6° 48'
11.	U 12 a 58 16	37°	3°	" "	1900^x	4° 16'
12.	U 12 c 50 30	50°	2°	" "	2800^x	8°
13.	U 11 d 33 68	86°	3°	" "	2400^x	[illegible]
14.	U 11 d 25 75	82°	5°	" "	2400^x	[illegible]

Note:- No 9 gun will vertically search between 2000^x & 2300^x
No 14 gun will not traverse to the left till Zero + 5

10. ACKNOWLEDGE.

Issued at 8 pm.
29-12-17.

[illegible signature]
Capt.
Comdg. 172 M.G. Coy.

Copy No 1 War Diary.
2 172nd Bde.
3 O.C. Operations.
4. D.M.G.O.
5, 6 & 7 Section Officers.

SECRET.

OPERATION ORDER "C"
by O.C. 172nd M.G.Coy.

1. The guns of the 172nd M.G. Coy. will be relieved on the evening of 1st Jan. 1918 by the guns of the 53rd and 55th M.G. Coys. as follows:-

55th M.G. Coy will relieve:-

No. of gun position.	Map Reference.	
1.	U 12 b 90 20	Right Sector
2	U 12 d 63 87	Right Sector
3	U 12 b 25 96	Right Sector
4	U 6 d 10 20	Right Sector
5	U 6 c 90 [illegible]	Left Sector
6	U 6 c 80 50	Left Sector
7	U 6 c 08 50	Left Sector
8	U 5 d 93 28	Left Sector
9	U 5 d 40 38	Left Sector
10	U 11 b 70 60	Left Sector
AA gun	U 12 b 20 90	

53rd M.G. Coy will relieve:-

11	U 12 c 68 18
12	U 12 c 50 30
13	U 11 d 35 68
14	U 11 d 23 75

2. Guides will be at Signal Farm for 53rd M.G. Coy at 2 p.m. and for 55th M.G. Coy at 3 p.m.

3. Headquarters of both 53rd & 55th Coys. will be at SIGNAL FARM.

4. Section Officers will personally report relief to Signal Farm as soon as possible.

5. 172nd M.G. Coy. will move to BOX CAMP A.5 c 1.9.

6. 2/Lieut. Barker will arrange for one limber to be at SIGNAL FARM at 4 p.m. and one at 7 p.m.

7. Relief complete will be reported to 172nd Bde. by BAB code.

8. ACKNOWLEDGE.

E. Needham Capt.
Comdg. 172nd M.G. Coy.

31-12-17.
Issued at 6 pm.

Copy. No. 1 War Diary.
2 172nd Bde.
3 53rd M.G. Coy
4. 55th M.G. Coy.
5 2/10 K.L.R.
6 2/4 S.L.R.
7. 8. & 9 Section Officers.
10 D.M.G.O.
11 & 12 Spare.

Instructions regarding War Diaries and Intelligence Summaries are contained in F. S. Regs., Part II. and the Staff Manual respectively. Title pages will be prepared in manuscript.

WAR DIARY
or
~~INTELLIGENCE SUMMARY.~~
(Erase heading not required.)

172nd M.G. Company

Army Form C. 2118.

Vol 12

Place	Date	Hour	Summary of Events and Information	Remarks and references to Appendices
BELGIUM Sheet 28. N.W.	1/1/18		The Coy was relieved in the line by the guns of the 53rd & 55th M.G. Coys – The Coy moved to BOX CAMP A5 c 1.9. 1 O.R to Hospital sick. 1 O.R returned from Hospital.	
	2/1/18		at 9.30 a.m the Coy paraded for baths.	
	3/1/18		Parades. 9.15 a.m Inspection by Section Officers – 9.30–10.30 a.m Squad Drill 10.30 12.30 p.m Cleaning of Camp. 2.15 p.m Care of Feet. The Transport paraded at 10 a.m to move by Road to the new area	
BELGIUM & FRANCE Sheet 36.	4/1/18		The Coy moved to STEENWERCK by rail entraining at INTERNATIONAL CORNER. The Coy was billeted in various houses with H^d Quarters at A.22 a 2-8 1 O.R to Hospital.	
	5/1/18		Lt Donaldson, 2nd Lts Ackroyd Nyryan & Jones with 3 O.Rs from each section reconnoitred the Reserve defences of ARMENTIERES. The Coy is under orders to occupy the M.G positions in this area at 20 minutes notice – Capt N S G^t MANSERGH rejoined the Coy and assumed temporary Command. 1 O.R returned from leave.	
	6/1/18		Church service at 10 a.m. 2nd Lt OAKESHOTT & 3 O.R's per section reconnoitred shortest route to PAVILION MUSICALE Sheet 36 N.W. H15 d 2 8 – the meeting place for the guides to take the Coy to gun positions in ARMENTIERES in case of attack. 1 O.R returned from Hospital.	

(A7092). Wt. W12839/M1293 750,000. 1/17. D. D. & L., Ltd. Forms/C.2118/14.

Instructions regarding War Diaries and Intelligence Summaries are contained in F. S. Regs., Part II. and the Staff Manual respectively. Title pages will be prepared in manuscript.

WAR DIARY
or
~~INTELLIGENCE~~ SUMMARY.
(Erase heading not required.)

Army Form C. 2118.

Place	Date	Hour	Summary of Events and Information	Remarks and references to Appendices
BELGIUM & FRANCE Sheet 36.	7/1/18		Parades. 9.15 am Section parade under Section Officers 9.30-10.30 am Section drill under Section Officers 10.30-11.30 am Inspection of SBRs & PHs 11.30-12.30 pm Care & cleaning – 2.0 pm Care of feet. 2nd Lt Vyvan & Oddershitt with 3 ORs of 1. 3 & 4 Sections reconnoitred the defences of ARMENTIERS 1 OR to Course of instruction at CAMIERS. 1 OR evacuated to CCS Capt G A WADE MC rejoined the Coy from A/DMGO and assumed command.	
	8/1/18		Parades. 9.15 am Sections parade under Section Officers 9.30-10.30 am Section drill. 10.30-11.30 am Belt Filling 11.30-12.30 pm Care & Cleaning – 2.0 pm Care of feet 2nd Lt Ackroyd & Jones reconnoitred the rear defences of ARMENTIERES with 3 ORs of Nos 1. 3 & 4 Sections	
	9/1/18		Parades 9.15 am Sections parade under Section Officers. 9.30-10.25 am Section drill. 10.25-11.00 am SBR drill 11-11.45 Belt Filling 11.45-12.30 pm Care & cleaning – 2 pm Care of feet. 2Lt W.G DONALDSON to Flying Course at BERTANGLES.	
	10/1/18		Parades 9.15 am Sections Parade under Section Officers. 9.30-10.15 am Section & Saluting drill 10.15-11 am SBR drill 11-11.45 Belt Filling 11.45. 12.30 pm Care & Cleaning. 2 pm Care of feet 19 ORs reported from 57th Div Dept Battn. Capt G A WADE MC and Capt N.S.St MANSERGH reconnoitred the rear defences of ARMENTIERES 2nd Lt O. GREENWOOD returned from leave to U.K. 1 OR to hospital.	
	11/1/18		Parades. 9.15 am Sections Parade under Section Officers. 9.30-10.30 am Section & Saluting drill. 10.30-11.30 Belt Filling 11.30-12.30 pm Care & cleaning – 2 pm Care of feet. 2nd Lts ACKROYD. GREENWOOD & JONES reconnoitred the M.G. emplacements in the ARMENTIERS sector. 2 ORs to Hospital	

(A7092). Wt. W12839/M1293. 750,000. 1/17. D. D. & L., Ltd. Forms/C.2118/14.

Instructions regarding War Diaries and Intelligence Summaries are contained in F. S. Regs., Part II. and the Staff Manual respectively. Title pages will be prepared in manuscript.

WAR DIARY
or
~~INTELLIGENCE~~ SUMMARY.

(*Erase heading not required.*)

Army Form C. 2118.

Place	Date	Hour	Summary of Events and Information	Remarks and references to Appendices
	12/1/18		The Coy paraded for Baths. In the afternoon Preparation for Trenches in the afternoon. 2. O.R's to Hospital.	
Ref: Maps HOUPLINES. BOIS. GRENIER	13/1/18		The Coy relieved the 171. M.G Coy in the line as per attached Operation order. Two O.R's to Hosp: Sick	
	14/1/18		Parades – Billet Fatigues – 1. O.R leave to U.K. Lt W.G DONALDSON returned from Flying Course – Indirect fire by night. 10,000 rounds being fired on the following targets Road I6a 15.50 – I6a 45.20. 7m & Tracks I12a 43.97 X Roads at WEZ MACQUART. FME DU CHASTEL. CENTURY TRENCH. TRAMWAY C30b 2.2.	
	15/1/18.		Parades – Billet Fatigues – 2. O.R's to Signalling Course – 1. O.R. to Hosp: Sick. Indirect fire by night 10250 rounds being fired on the following targets. Road I6a 45.20 Rd & TRAMWAY I7d 95.47 Rd WEZ MACQUART. I23a 40.30 INANE AV: I12a 60.27 to I12b 30.97 7m & TRACKS I12a 43.97 Rd at I7b 65.30 X Roads WEZ MACQUART. CENTURY TRENCH TRAMWAY C30b 2.2. – RAILWAY I12b 06.70.	
	16/1/18.		Parades details at H.Q for baths. LT. W.G DONALDSON to Hospital. Indirect fire carried out by night on the following targets 9000 rounds being fired: RUINS I6a 5.1 Rd & TRAMWAY I7d 95.37 INANE AVE I12a 60.97 – I12b 30.97 TRAMWAY Rd & DUG OUTS at C24c 55.10 DUMP I12b 95.75 X Roads. WEZ MACQUART. LE TEMPLE C30d 9.0. L'AVENTURE C30a 80.03 TRAMWAY JUNC: at C30b 2.2 RAILWAY HALT I12d 06.70	

(A7092). Wt. W12839/M1293. 750,000. 1/17. D. D. & L., Ltd. Forms/C.2118/14.

Army Form C. 2118.

Instructions regarding War Diaries and Intelligence Summaries are contained in F. S. Regs., Part II. and the Staff Manual respectively. Title pages will be prepared in manuscript.

WAR DIARY

~~or~~

~~INTELLIGENCE SUMMARY.~~

(Erase heading not required.)

Place	Date	Hour	Summary of Events and Information	Remarks and references to Appendices
REF. MAPS. HOUPLINES & BOIS. GRENIER. 1:10.000.	17/1/18		Parades : Billet Fatigues C.S.M. EMMOTT returned from leave 15/1/18. 1.O.R. to Hosp: Sick 1.O.R. to GRANTHAM for special course. Indirect fire carried out by night on the following targets 16000 rounds being fired. I5b70.90 to I6a75.00 INANE DRIVE. INANE ALLEY. X Roads WEZ MACQUART LETEMPLE C30d 9.0 L'AVENTURE C30a 80.03. TRAMWAY Junc: C30b2.2. C24A 40.50 C24b00.00 RAILWAY HALT I12d 56.70 —	
	18/1/18		Parades. Billet Fatigues 1.O.R to Hosp. sick 3 OR's evacuated — Indirect fire carried out by night on the following targets 9350 rounds being fired on the following targets. RUINS. I6a 5.1. TRAMWAY RUELLE de la NOIX I17b 25.10. Road I12b 17.00 I12c 90.30 TRAMWAY Rd and DUGOUT C24c 56.05. JUNCTION of INCARNATION AVENUE and Rd I17b 65.30 X Roads. WEZ MACQUART CENTRAL DRIVE. C30c 0.5 to C30c 25.35 Houses C30d 50.50 TRAMWAY JUNC: C30b 2.2 LA FRESNELLE X Roads C12b 9.6.	
	19/1/18		Parades — Billet Fatigues. 1.O.R leave to U.K. 21/1/18 — 4/2/18 — Indirect fire carried out by night on the following targets 9000 rounds being fired. RUINS at I6a 5.1. I5b 70.90 — TRAMWAY RUELLE DE LA VOIX I17b 25.10. ROAD I12b 17.00 to I12c 90.30 Junc: of INCARNATE AVE and Rd at I17b 65.30 X ROADS WEZ. MACQUART. LETEMPLE C30d 9.0 TRENCH. C30d 7.1 to I6b 70.60. LEFALUT TRAMWAY JUNC: D25a 60.80 X Roads LA FRESNELLE I12b 95.85.	

(A7092). Wt. W12839/M1293. 750,000. 1/17. D. D. & L., Ltd. Forms/C.2118/14.

Army Form C. 2118.

WAR DIARY
or
INTELLIGENCE SUMMARY.
(Erase heading not required.)

Instructions regarding War Diaries and Intelligence Summaries are contained in F. S. Regs., Part II. and the Staff Manual respectively. Title pages will be prepared in manuscript.

Place	Date	Hour	Summary of Events and Information	Remarks and references to Appendices
	20/1/18		Parades Billet Fatigues - Indirect fire carried out at night on the following targets 8000 rounds being fired - RUINS at I6a. 5.1 - TRAMWAY RUELLE de la MX I17b 25.10 ROAD I12b 17.00 to I12c 90.30 JUNCTION of INCARN: AVE and ROAD I17b 65.30 LE TEMPLE C30d 9.0 TRENCH FROM C30d 7.1 to I6b 7.6 LE FALOT TRAMWAY JUNC D25a 60.80 RAILWAY HALT I12d 02.70. LT P McGRATH & LT N E DONALDSON having been evacuated out of the Corps are are struck off the strength accordingly. 1 OR to hospital sick.	
Ref Map. BELGIUM & FRANCE Sheet 36.	21/1/18		The 171st M G Coy relieved the 172nd M G Coy in the line; the latter proceeded to billets at A22a 3.7. No: 123387 Pte PEELING A.G died of wounds received in action on 20/1/18 -	
	22/1/18		Parade. 9.30 am Inspection by Section officers and cleaning up - 2nd Lt GADD returned from leave.	
	23/1/18		Parade 9.30 am Inspection by Section officers and cleaning up. 1 O R to hospital sick.	
	24/1/18		Parade 9.30 am. Inspection by section officers and cleaning up. 4 O R's to hospital sick.	
	25/1/18		Parade Inspection of the Coy by the O.C. - 4 O R's to hospital sick ~~1 O R [illegible]~~	
	26/1/18		Parade - The Coy paraded for Baths at 8.30. a.m. Blankets disinfected. 6 reinforcements arrived. 2 O.R's to hospital sick, 1 O.R evacuated	

(A7092). Wt. W12839/M1293. 750,000. 1/17. D. D. & L., Ltd. Forms/C.2118/14.

Army Form C. 2118.

Instructions regarding War Diaries and Intelligence Summaries are contained in F. S. Regs., Part II. and the Staff Manual respectively. Title pages will be prepared in manuscript.

WAR DIARY

~~or~~

~~INTELLIGENCE SUMMARY.~~

(Erase heading not required.)

Place	Date	Hour	Summary of Events and Information	Remarks and references to Appendices
Ref – Maps HOUPLINES and BOIS GRENIER.	27-1-18		Parades. 8.45 am move to trenches. 172 M.G.C. relieved 171 M.G.C. in ARMENTIERES Sector as per relief Orders herewith. 1 O.R. to hospital sick. 1 O.R. from Hospital. Cpl Conway deprived of Lance stripe. 2nd Lt D. G. GREEN reported from M.G.C. Base Depot.	
	28-1-18.		Parades: 9-15 Inspection: 9-45 Billet fatigues. 11-0 Close order drill. 11-30 S.B.R. drill. 12-0 Cleaning gun Kit 2-0 Care of feet. ~~All 4 Sects in the line – 5 men per team. Indirect fire carried out on INANE AV, LA BLUE, Road junction WEZ MACQUART, GAPS in enemy wire.~~	
	29-1-18		Parades: Baths for details + H.Q. 2-0 Care of feet. Capt MANSERGH leave to U.K. 1 O.R. awarded 7 days F.P. No 2. Indirect fire on Gaps in enemy wire, INANE AVENUE, LA BLEUE, LE FALOT, Road junction WEZ MACQUART.	
	30-1-18.		Parades: 9-15 Inspection. 9-30 Billet fatigues. 2-0 Care of feet. Indirect fire carried out on Gaps in enemy wire, LE TEMPLE C30 d 9.0, Tram and Road junction L'AVENTURE C30. a 85.05. LE FALOT, Tram junction D25 a 68. 60. Road + Tramway WEZ MACQUART, LA BLEUE, INANE AVENUE. 11,250 rounds were fired. Intended raid on enemy trenches cancelled until tomorrow.	

J. Greenwood 2Lt.
for O.C. 172 Machine Gun Coy.

(A7092). Wt. W12839/M1293. 750,000. 1/17. D. D. & L., Ltd. Forms/C.2118/14.

SECRET

Relief of 171st Machine Gun Coy

Map reference: ARMENTIERES 1/10,000
BOIS GRENIER 1/10,000

1. By daylight on the morning of the 13th inst. the 173 [illegible] Coy will relieve the 171st M.G.Coy in the [illegible] section.
2. Each section of this Company will relieve the section [illegible] the [illegible] number in the 171st M.G.Coy and gun positions [illegible] [illegible] as set forth in [illegible] in that Company.
3. Tripods, belt boxes etc. will not be taken over. Each section will arrange to take in the [illegible] [illegible] [illegible] [illegible] each as follows:-

[illegible]
[illegible]
[illegible]
[illegible]
[illegible]
Spare parts box.

4. Each gun team will consist of 4 men & 1 N.C.O. [illegible] [illegible] up to this strength under section arrangements. Remainder of personnel will remain at Company H.Qrs. As soon as possible after the guides [illegible] will report to Coy H.Qrs. [illegible] [illegible] [illegible] [illegible] [illegible] [illegible] & where they are to be [illegible] [illegible] [illegible] [illegible] [illegible] guide to conduct section leader to [illegible] [illegible] [illegible] [illegible] one to guide section leader to SQUARE FARM. [illegible] [illegible] [illegible] Coy H.Q. at 4:30 p.m. on 13th inst.
5. No [illegible] of any description will be [illegible] [illegible] [illegible]. Particulars of [illegible] [illegible] [illegible] [illegible] [illegible] to Coy H.Qrs. as soon as possible after [illegible].
6. A report on standing [illegible] [illegible] [illegible] [illegible] [illegible] [illegible] [illegible] [illegible] [illegible] [illegible] [illegible] [illegible] [illegible]
7. Advance parties of [illegible] [illegible] [illegible] [illegible] [illegible] [illegible] [illegible] Lt. Schorge on 12th inst. immediately after [illegible] [illegible] [illegible]. [illegible] will make all arrangements for the party. [illegible] Officer [illegible] [illegible] [illegible] [illegible] [illegible] [illegible] [illegible] [illegible] to Coy H.Qrs. Lt. Schorge will arrange for [illegible] [illegible] [illegible] [illegible] [illegible] [illegible] [illegible] [illegible] [illegible] 12th inst.
8. No man will be [illegible] [illegible] the [illegible] [illegible] [illegible] [illegible] [illegible] [illegible] change of [illegible] on the 12th inst.
9. [illegible] will be left at Coy H.Qrs. [illegible] [illegible] [illegible] [illegible] [illegible] [illegible] [illegible] [illegible] [illegible] [illegible] [illegible] [illegible] [illegible] [illegible] [illegible] left at Coy H.Qrs.
10. Following is a list of gun positions, sections finding the guns, officers in charge

POSITION	SECTION BY WHICH GUN IS FOUND	OFFICER RESPONSIBLE	OFFICER'S BILLET
C.23 b 75.33	1	Lt. Schorge	FUSILIER LANE
C.27 [illegible] 63.86	1	do.	do.
C.[illegible] 50.39	1	do.	do.
C.22 [illegible] 60.00	1	Lt. [illegible]	[illegible]
I 4 b 33.86	2	Lt. [illegible]	[illegible]
I 3 d 49.02	2	do.	do.
I 3 [illegible] 95.93	2	do.	do.
I [illegible] 57.75	2	do.	do.
I 10 [illegible] 02.05	3	Lt. [illegible]	[illegible]
I 10 3 56.05	3	do.	do.
I 7 [illegible] [illegible]	3	do.	do.
C 27 c 56.40	4	Lt. [illegible]	[illegible]
C 28 c [illegible]	4	do.	do.
C 22 c [illegible]	4	do.	do.
I 4 [illegible] 63.55	4	Lt. [illegible]	[illegible]

11. Section officers will personally inspect all [illegible] on 12th inst. before these men go into the [illegible] the prospect of [illegible] attacks [illegible]

12. Every detachment will be provided with written orders for their new position which must be known [illegible]

13. Transport Officer will arrange to take over [illegible] by 171st M. G. Coy. [illegible] will report to O.C. at [illegible] a.m. each day

14. On the 12th inst. [illegible] will be left [illegible] It will be responsible for the [illegible] to the officer from 171st M.G. Coy. [illegible] Company will parade [illegible] ready to march to the [illegible] of the relief. [illegible] will be [illegible] a.m.

15. Relief will be reported complete by [illegible] to [illegible] H.Q. [illegible]

16. ACKNOWLEDGE.

[illegible] Major.
O.C. 172 M.G. Coy.

Distribution.

1. [illegible]
2. [illegible]
3. 171st M. G. Coy.
4. O.C.
5. [illegible]
6. [illegible]
7. [illegible]
8. [illegible]
9. [illegible]
10. Transport Officer
11. [illegible]
12. [illegible]

SECRET.

Copy No 2.

Relief Orders.

1. On 21st Jan. 1918 the 172nd M.G. Coy. will be relieved by 141st M.G. Coy. in the ARMENTIERES Sector.

2. Belt boxes & tripods will be handed over to incoming unit who will leave an equivalent number at Coy H.Qrs. on their way to the line.

3. Relieving company will leave Coy. H.Qrs. at 11.30 a.m. & limbers will bring back material of this Company.

4. All particulars with reference to [illegible] will be handed over most fully.

5. Emplacements, dugouts & latrines will be left perfectly clean.
Certificates will be obtained by each section officer to this effect and handed to the O.C. at Coy. H.Qrs. before relief, also receipts in duplicate for all trench stores handed over.

6. After relief sections will return to Coy. H.Qrs. & will there receive further instructions as to proceeding to billets in the STEENWERCK area.

7. No guides will be required by 141st M.G. Coy.

8. Transport Officer will arrange for limbers to attend Coy. H.Q. to convey guns & material to STEENWERCK area at 3 p.m.

9. Pack ponies will be kept by 141st Coy. at their present transport lines STEENWERCK & by 172nd Coy. at the transport lines at PONT NIEPPE.
Transport Officer will be responsible that S.A.A. at STEENWERCK is checked on arrival there.

10. All details with regard to Q.M. Stores, [illegible] will be arranged by 2 i/c.

11. One house in ARMENTIERES is permanently allotted for sole use of this Company and one for sole use of 141st M.G. Coy. All [illegible] not likely to be needed at STEENWERCK during next few days will be dumped there.

12. Ptes. Abbott, Trumble, [illegible] and Jones ([illegible]) will remain in that house and will be rationed by 172nd M.G. Coy.

13. 2 i/c will be responsible for [illegible] so that he can in absence of O.C. who will stay two days in ARMENTIERES, act in any emergency.

14. ACKNOWLEDGE.

[illegible] Capt.
for O.C. 172 M.G. Coy

Distribution.

Copy No 1 172nd Inf. Bde.
2 War Diary ✓
3 [illegible]
4 2 i/c
5 O.C. No 1 Section.
6 " 2 "
7 " 3 "
8 " 4 "
9 O.C. [illegible] M.G. Coy
10 " 141st M.G. Coy
11 [illegible] M.G. Coy
12 [illegible]
13 } Spare
14 }

13.

26-1-18

[illegible]

6. [illegible]

7. [illegible]

[illegible] duties are:—

a. To maintain a supply of [illegible] [illegible]

b. To see that [illegible]

(1) [illegible]

(2) [illegible]

(3) [illegible]

(4) [illegible]

(5) [illegible]

(6) [illegible]

(7) [illegible]

(8) [illegible]

8. If any man is showing signs of [illegible] [illegible] at the [illegible] [illegible] to the O.C. [illegible] [illegible]

9. No [illegible] must be made by the [illegible]

10. O.C. Sections are responsible for [illegible]

11. Every man will [illegible] to the [illegible]

12. [illegible]

13. [illegible] may be used [illegible] the night. They will be [illegible] will be returned as soon as possible [illegible]

[illegible]

Instructions regarding War Diaries and Intelligence Summaries are contained in F. S. Regs., Part II. and the Staff Manual respectively. Title pages will be prepared in manuscript.

WAR DIARY
or
INTELLIGENCE SUMMARY.
(Erase heading not required.)

172 M.G.C.

Army Form C. 2118.

Place	Date	Hour	Summary of Events and Information	Remarks and references to Appendices
Ref - MAPS. HOUPLINES and BOIS GRENIER	Feby 1.		Parades. Preparation for move + billet fatigues 9-0am. Baths. ~~No 1 Section on the LAUNDRIES, ERQUINGHEM under D.M.G.O.~~ The M.G's took part in Barrage for raid by 2/9 K.L.R. Enemy lines raided between I17a 08.50 and I17a 20.70. Strength of raiding party 3 off 100 O.R's. Raid successful capturing 6 prisoners 2 being disposed of on the way back. Our casualties NIL. Operation Order attached. 1 O.R. to Chiropodist's course. 1 O.R. leave to U.K.	No 1.
	Feby 2		171 M.G. Coy relieved this Coy by daylight. No 1 Section took up the following defensive positions in ARMENTIERES:- FARM POST, HERRING CORNER, DURHAM CASTLE, and JAMES CORNER. This Section was attached to 173 M.G. Coy. Belt boxes + Tripods were handed over.	No 2
	Feby 3.		Coy in billets in STEENWERK. Parades 9-30 Inspection + cleaning up. 1 O.R. to 51 C.C.S. 2 O.Rs wounded in action on the 1st and 2nd inst	
	Feby 4		Parades 9-30 Inspection + cleaning up. 1 O.R. from hospital.	
	Feby 5		172 M.G. Coy relieved the 171 M.G. Coy in the ARMENTIERES Section - 8 guns. 4 guns of 172 M.G. Coy relieved 4 guns of the 173 M.G. Coy at BOULOGNE, FOLKESTONE, SIBERIA, and HELENE positions in ARMENTIERES. 4 guns of 171 M.G. Coy relieved 4 guns of 172 M.G. Coy in HOUPLINES. No 1 Section moved to the LAUNDRIES in ERQUINGHEM under D.M.G.O. The 172 Inf Bde took over the ARMENTIERES Section and 171 Inf Bde the HOUPLINES Section. Indirect fire was carried out on X roads WEZ MACQUART, TRAMWAYS and ROADS. 6000 rounds were fired. 2 O.R. to hospital.	No 3.

(A7092). Wt. W12839/M1293. 750,000. 1/17. D. D. & L., Ltd. Forms/C.2118/14.

Army Form C. 2118.

Instructions regarding War Diaries and Intelligence Summaries are contained in F. S. Regs., Part II. and the Staff Manual respectively. Title pages will be prepared in manuscript.

WAR DIARY
or
INTELLIGENCE SUMMARY.
(Erase heading not required.)

Place	Date	Hour	Summary of Events and Information	Remarks and references to Appendices
Ref - Maps. HOUPLINES and BOIS GRENIER.	Feby 6.		3 Sections in the line - Nos 2, 3 & 4. Coy H.Q. at H.6a 10.99. Machine guns took part in barrage for raid on enemy trenches at C 29 a 45.10. to C 29 a 60.50 by the 2/7 K.L.R. Raid was very successful capturing 10 prisoners and a light German M.G. Our casualties were slight. Parades: 9-15 Inspection - drill order. 9-45 Billet fatigues. 1 O.R wounded.	No 4.
	Feby 7.		No 3 Section relieved No 4 Section in the line. The 2 support line guns were standing-to expecting a Bosch raid on our Nos 1 and 2 posts in front line. Parades: 9-15 Inspection. 9.45 Fatigues. 2.15 foot washing. Indirect fire on TRAMWAYS, DUMPS and ROADS. 6000 rounds were fired	
	Feby 8.		The 2 support guns still standing to. Parades 9.0 Inspection; 9-15 Fatigues. Indirect fire on same targets - 6000 rounds were fired. 3 O.Rs leave to U.K., 1 Officer 1 O.R. to 2nd Army Central School for course. 1 O.R from CAMIERES course; 1 O.R. from hospital. 1 O.R. from leave. 1st Army Trench Standing Orders taken into effect by this Coy.	
	Feby 9.		The 2 support guns still standing to. Parades 9-15 Inspection; 9-30 fatigues 2-15 washing & care of feet. Indirect fire on usual targets - 4000 rounds were fired. 2 O.R. to 54 C.C.S.	

(A7092). Wt. W12839/M1293. 750,000. 1/17. D. D. & L., Ltd. Forms/C.2118/14.

Instructions regarding War Diaries and Intelligence Summaries are contained in F. S. Regs., Part II. and the Staff Manual respectively. Title pages will be prepared in manuscript.

WAR DIARY
or
INTELLIGENCE SUMMARY.
(Erase heading not required.)

Army Form C. 2118.

Place	Date	Hour	Summary of Events and Information	Remarks and references to Appendices
Ref - Maps. HOUPLINES and BOIS GRENIER.	Feby 10		The support line guns still standing to. Parades: 9.15 Inspection, 9-30 Fatigues; 2-15 Care of feet. Indirect fire on same targets - 4000 rounds being fired. 2 O.R. to hospital 1 O.R. from hospital. 1 O.R. to 54 C.C.S. Cpl Robinson transferred from No 4 Sect to No 2 Sect. The following promotions were made:- L/Cpl Derrick to Cpl, L/Cpl Densley to be paid L/Cpl. Pte Lowe to L/Cpl unpaid.	
	Feby 11		The support line guns still standing to. Parades 8-30 - Baths; 2-0 Inspection in full marching order. Usual indirect fire carried out - 6000 rounds were fired. 2Lt GREEN relieved 2Lt OAKESHOTT.	
	Feby 12		The support line guns still standing to. Parades: 9-15 Inspection - 9-30 Fatigues - 2-15 Care of feet. Usual indirect fire carried out - 6000 rounds were fired. L/Cpl A. Wright awarded the Croix de Guerre. D.R.O. 156. 1 O.R. from hospital.	
	Feby 13.		The support line guns still standing to. Parades. 9-0 Inspection, 9-15 Fatigues. 2-15 Care of feet. Usual indirect fire carried out - 6000 rounds were fired. 2 O.R. from signalling course. Following punishments awarded - Ptes Jackson & Woods. 3 days F.P. No 2. Pte Manson, 7 days F.P. No 1.	

(A7092). Wt. W12839/M1293. 750,000. 1/17. D. D. & L., Ltd. Forms/C.2118/14.

Instructions regarding War Diaries and Intelligence Summaries are contained in F. S. Regs., Part II. and the Staff Manual respectively. Title pages will be prepared in manuscript.

WAR DIARY
or
INTELLIGENCE SUMMARY.
(Erase heading not required.)

Army Form C. 2118.

Place	Date	Hour	Summary of Events and Information	Remarks and references to Appendices
Ref - Maps. HOUPLINES and BOIS GRENIER. Sheet 36A N.E.	Feby 14		172 M.G. Coy were relieved by the 113 M.G. Coy. The Coy moved into Corps reserve at NEUF BERQUIN. Map ref of H.Q. Sheet 36A N.E. L 25 a 70.95. 1 O.R. from course. 1 O.R. to 51 C.C.S. 4 O.R. leave. 1 O.R. to CAMIERES	No 5.
	Feby 15		Parades 9-30 Inspection & cleaning up. 2-0 Care of feet. 57 M.G. Batt formed under Command of Lt Col. J.F.R. HOPE, D.S.O. Capt MANSERGH appointed Adjutant for Batt. Whilst in Corps Reserve the Coy are responsible for the Machine Gun Defence of the points detailed in Operation Order No 12 herewith, in case of an enemy attack on the Portuguese.	No 6
	Feby 16		Parades: 9-0 Inspection by Section Officers. 11-0 Coy with transport parade for inspection by O.C. Coy. 2-0 Care of feet. 3 O.R. to hospital	
	Feby 17		Parades: 9-30 Inspection by Section Officers. 2-0 Care of feet. 3-0 C. of E. Service in transport billet. Small Kit inspection by Section Officers. Sick parade 7-45 am at Batt H.Q. Fire piquet detailed each day and fire appliances kept at Coy H.Q. 3 O.R. to hospital. 2 O.R. on leave to U.K.	
	Feby 18		Parades 7-45 Inspection by Section Officers. 9-0 am Coy paraded to reconnoitre the defensive positions mentioned in Operation Order No 12. Guns were also taken and tested in each emplacement. C.O's lecture at Batt H.Q. to Officers & N.C.O's at 5-30 pm. Whilst in Corps Reserve feet only to be rubbed on alternate days instead of every day. 1 Officer & 1 O.R. leave to U.K. The following classes assemble daily at Batt H.Q. Rangefinding, Signalling and Drill	

Army Form C. 2118.

Instructions regarding War Diaries and Intelligence Summaries are contained in F. S. Regs., Part II. and the Staff Manual respectively. Title pages will be prepared in manuscript.

WAR DIARY
or
INTELLIGENCE SUMMARY.
(Erase heading not required.)

Place	Date	Hour	Summary of Events and Information	Remarks and references to Appendices
Ref - Maps Sheet 36A N.E.	Feby 19		Parades: 7.45 Inspection by Section Officers; 9-0 to 10-0 Squad drill + rifle exercises; 10-0-11-0 Classes; 11-0 to 11-15 Break; 11-15-11-45 Musketry; 11-45-1-0 Elementary gun drill; 2-0-2-45 Care + cleaning of guns + limbers. 2-45-3-0 Care of feet 3-0 games. 1 O.R. from leave. 1 N.C.O. rejoined Coy from base. 1 N.C.O. from Base depot. Following punishments awarded: L/Cpl Small deprived lance stripe; 2 O.R's awarded 3 days F.P. No 1; 1 O.R. awarded 5 days F.P. No 2.	
	Feby 20		Parades 7.45 Inspection by Section Officers: 9-30 parade for baths; 2-30 care and cleaning; 3-0 Games. Lecture at Cinema MERVILLE by Mr Bennett at 3-0. 25 O.R's attended. Cpl Tyrer transferred from H.Q. to No 3 Section.	
	Feby 21		Parades: 7.45 Inspection by Section Officers; 9-10 Squad drill; 10-11 Classes; 11-11.15 Break; 11-15-11-45 Musketry; 11-45-12 30 Elementary gun drill; 2-2.45 Care + cleaning; 2.45-3.0 Care of feet; 3-0 Games. Lt YVYAN + 1 O.R. to hospital + struck off the strength of the Coy. Major W. R. GRIERSON, D.S.O. assumes the duties of Second in Command to the Batt.	
	Feby 22		Parades 7.45 Inspection by Section Officers; 9-0-10.0 Saluting drill; 10-11 Classes; 11-11.15 Break; 11-15-11-45 Musketry; 11-45-12 30 "Action" drill; 2-2.45 Care + cleaning 2.45 Games. 3 O.R. evacuated to Base.	
	Feby 23		Parades: 7.45 Inspection by Section Officers; 9-10 Company drill; 10-11 Action from improvised pack saddles by Batt T.O. 11-11.15 Break; 11-15-11-45 Musketry; 11-45-12.30 Action from pack saddles; 2-2.45 Care + cleaning; 2.45-3-0 Care of feet; 3-0 Games: 1 O.R. to hospital. 20 O.R's attached to this Coy from the Infantry were transferred to this Coy. Batt canteen opened under Sgt Newton. 1 O.R. attached to Batt H.Q.	

(A7092). Wt. W12839/M1293. 750,000. 1/17. D. D. & L., Ltd. Forms/C.2118/14.

Army Form, C. 2118.

Instructions regarding War Diaries and Intelligence Summaries are contained in F. S. Regs., Part II. and the Staff Manual respectively. Title pages will be prepared in manuscript.

WAR DIARY
or
INTELLIGENCE SUMMARY.
(Erase heading not required.)

Place	Date	Hour	Summary of Events and Information	Remarks and references to Appendices
Ref – Maps Sheet 36ᴬ N.E.	Feby 24		Parades: 9-0 Coy parade for Kit inspection; 2-45 R.C. church parade; 2-30 C. of E. church parade; 3 O.R's from leave; 3 reinforcements reported; 1 O.R. to hospital. 2 O.R. struck off the strength. C.Q.M.S. attended a meeting at Batt H.Q.	
	Feby 25		Parades: 7-45 Inspection by Section Officers; 9-0-9-45 Drill & P.T.; 9-45-10-30 Classes; 10-30-11 Musketry; 11-0-11-15 Break; 11-15-12-30 I.A.; 2-0-2-45 Care & cleaning; 2-45-3-0 Care of feet; 3-0 Games; 8 men for 3 days scouting course under 2Lt Gadd. Men for Batt classes detailed. Lecture by 2nd i/c Batt to Officers & N.C.O's. Subject "A machine Gun Coy in action." Class for Officers in the use of the Barr & Stroud under Batt 2i/c at 2-30. T.O. and T. Sgt attend at Batt H.Q. for instruction in Drill.	
	Feby 26		Parades: 8-30 Miniature range for Musketry – Grouping & application; 11-15-12-30 I.A.; 2-0-2-45 Care & cleaning; 2-45 Games; 2 N.C.O's to Batt for a 3 days course. 1 O.R. from hospital.	
	Feby 27		Parades: 8-0 Coy parade for baths; 2-2-45 Care & cleaning; 2-45 Games: This Coy is now known as No 3 Coy, 57 Div. M.G. Batt and the Sections lettered A.B.C. & D. 2Lt GREENWOOD O. appointed 2i/c of this Coy.	
	Feby 28		Parades: 7-45 Inspection by Section Officers; 9-9-45 Drill & P.T.; 9-45-10-30 Classes; 10-30-11 Musketry; 11-11-15 Break; 11-15-12-30 T.O.E.T. 2-0-2-45 Care & cleaning; 2-45 Games. 1 officer & 3 O.R's on leave; 1 O.R. to course of cold shoeing at ABBEVILLE. 1 O.R. to hospital. Lecture at Batt for Officers & N.C.O's	

[Signature] Capt
Comndg, 172nd Mg Coy

(A7092). Wt. W12839/M1293. 750,000. 1/17. D. D. & L., Ltd. Forms/C.2118/14.

SECRET

No 6

Copy No. [illegible]

Ref.
Map 36 N.W. 1:20,000.
36 S.E. 1:20,000.
Special Map attached.

Operation Order No. 12

172nd Machine Gun Company. 19.2.1918.

1. In the event of an enemy attack on the Portuguese the 172nd M.G. Coy is responsible for the Machine Gun Defence of the points detailed in table below:-

SECTION	NAME OF POSITION	APPROXIMATE MAP REF.	RESERVE SAA. IN POSITION	RESERVE SAA. to be taken	BATTLE LINE	SECTION H.Qrs.
1.	COLKSHY HOUSE.	M9b99	NIL	5,000.	125° G.	
1.	Do. Do.		NIL	5.000.	175° G.	CARTER POST M2c7.3.
1.	CARTER POST	M2c7.3.	5,000.	NIL.	90° G.	
1.	Do. Do.		5.000.	NIL.	190° G.	
2.	LE DRUMEZ.	M3c20.95.			160° G.	
2.	Do.		NIL.	5.000.	35° G.	LE DRUMEZ.
2.	MUDDY LANE	G33c15.15.			160° G.	
2.	Do.				25° G.	
3.	NOUVEAU MONDE.	G33a2.9			178° G.	NOUVEAU
3.	Do. Do.	G27c7.2.	NIL.	5.000.	145° G.	
3.	PONT LEVIS	G26c5.6.			203° G.	MONDE.
3.	CROSS ROADS.	R5a7.0.			NONE.	
4.	FOUR GUNS IN RESERVE AT G 32a 1.6.					

2. The above positions have been reconnoitred by all officers and O.R responsible for their occupation in case of alarm and a gun has been tested in each emplacement.

3. Upon receipt of the order "Defence Scheme MOVE" Sections will proceed independently with all speed to occupy the positions detailed in above table, where they will relieve XV Corps Cyclists, who will return to ESTAIRES.

After being unloaded limbers will proceed to Company H.Qrs G32a1.1. under arrangements to be made by Transport Officer.

4. Fighting limbers will always be packed ready for this move. Guns filled and the S.A.A. detailed in table in addition to 16 Belt Boxes per gun, will be placed in each fighting limber.

5. Transport Officer will arrange always to have immediately available mules and drivers for eight fighting limbers.

6. If, on arrival at gun positions the situation is uncertain scouts will at once be sent forward to see what is happening. In any case as soon as ESTAIRES is reached scouts, moving in pairs, will precede each two guns.

7. As the field of view from most emplacements is obscured by herbage a lookout will be posted to control the fire of the gun from near the emplacements.

8. In the event of these dispositions being taken up Company H.Qrs. will be at G32a11 LA BELLE CROIX. As soon as guns are in position two runners from each section will be sent to Company H.Q.

9. Should it for any reason be impossible to occupy the emplacements detailed gun commanders will fight their guns according to the tactical situation, making use of natural features and reporting their location to Coy. H.Qrs.

10. All guns, with exception of PONT LEVIS and CROSSROADS will have strong infantry support.

11. ACKNOWLEDGE.

Issued at 11 am 20:2:1918.

C.A. Wise
Capt
Comndg 172nd M.G. Coy

Copy No. 1 to 172nd Inf. Bde.
" " 2 57th Mc. G. Btn.
" " 3 170th M. G. Coy.
" " 4 O.C. No. 1 Section.
" " 5 do. 2 do.
" " 6 do. 3 do.
" " 7 do. 4 do
" " 8 Transport Officer.
" " 9 } War Diary
" " 10 }
" " 11 O.C. 9th KLR.
" " 12-14. Spare.

This is to certify that all dugouts, emplacements, cookhouses, latrines etc. at position were handed over by 172 M. G. Coy. to 113 M. G. Coy in a clean and sanitary condition.

Signed ____________

113 M. G. Coy.

This is to certify that all dugouts, emplacements, cookhouses, latrines etc. at position were handed over by 172 M. G. Coy to 113 M. G. Coy in a clean and sanitary condition.

Signed ____________

113 M. G. Coy

No 1

SECRET   Operation Order No. 10, 172nd M.G. Coy.   Copy No. ...

1. The 2/4th K.L.R. will raid enemy's lines between I.17a 05.50. and I.17a 20.70. at ZERO hour on 31st inst. Zero hour will be notified later. Approximate strength of raiding party 3 officers & 100 O.R. The barrage will be produced by Machine Guns, Artillery and Trench Mortars. Thirty five machine guns will be used.

2. The guns of 172nd M.G. Coy. will fire as under the moment the artillery barrage is put down at ZERO hour.

Guns	Map Ref.	Direction GRID.	Elevation	Target	Times & Rates of Fire
SQUARE FARM	I.9 d 11.02.	117°	4° 32'	I.17a 70.20.	ZERO – ZERO + 5 250 per min.
HALT	I.9 b 37.36.	125½°	6° 0'	I.17d 05.40.	
RAILWAY	I.3 d 41.02.	128°	8° 43'	I.17d 65.75.	
SALIENT	I.3 d 07.95	136°	7° 51'	I.17b 26.10.	
QUALITY.	I.4 a 57.76.	145°-149°	9° 11'	I.17b 36.15 to I.17b 66.35	ZERO + 5 till ZERO + 50 50 per min.
BUTERNE	I.4 a 65.57.	143½°	9° 40'	I.17b 90.50.	(ZERO for the Machine Guns is the moment our artillery barrage comes down.)
DISTILLERY.	C.28 c 63.44	151½°	10° 42'	I.17b 30.60.	
CEMETERY.	C.28 c 52.66.	153°	7° 51'	I.11c 97.12.	

3. Each Section Officer will detail a runner to be at O.C. Coy.'s Battalion dugout in HEADQUARTERS WALK at ZERO – 60 mins.

4. Watches will be synchronized at Btn. H.Qrs. of 2/4 K.L.R. Subsidiary Line at 2.10 pm 31/1/18.

5. The following code will be used in connection with this raid :–

Operations postponed 30 minutes.... CABBAGE.
Operation cancelled .... POTATO.
Have formed up .... CRESS.
Raid successful .... MUSTARD.
All going well .... CELERY.
Much resistance .... BEANS.
Weak do. .... PEAS.
Prisoners returning .... SEEDS.
Many casualties .... ONIONS.
Few do. .... TOMATO.
Held up .... LETTUCE.
Party all in .... CARROT.

Artillery and Machine Guns to continue an extra 10 minutes viz ZERO+50 to ZERO+60 .. CUCUMBER.

No reference to this operation is to be made on telephone previous to ZERO.

6. Rifle Grenade bursting into 2 REDS and 2 WHITES will be the signal for the Artillery and M.G. Barrage to continue an extra 10 minutes. This signal will be sent up by O.C. Raid and repeated at Coy. & Btn. H.Qrs.
All gun teams must keep a careful lookout for this signal.

7. The Raiding Party will penetrate to dugouts at I 17a 22.36., I 17a 29.44 and I 17a 33.52. On Z night No. 2 Post, Front Line, (MUSHROOM) will be evacuated until hostile barrage has died down; front line posts will be thinned down or withdrawn.

8. O.C. No. 3 Section & O.C. No. 1 Section will detail a runner to be at Right & Left Btn. HQrs respectively to convey to them any telephone messages.

9. In the event of communication breaking down gun commanders will conform to the action of our Artillery.

10. All communications after ZERO - 1 hour to COY. H.Q. HEADQUARTERS WALK I 19c 70.55.

11. Guns must be carefully laid & ready for checking by C.O. at ZERO - 30 mins.

12. O.C. Sections will make their own arrangements for supplies of S.A.A., water, oil etc.

13. All guns will be fitted with an adequate Depression Stop.

14. Before ZERO usual indirect fire will be carried out.

15. After firing the barrage guns will remain in position ready to put down another barrage if called for till ZERO + 120 mins. Guns will then be laid on usual S.O.S. lines & the ordinary programme of indirect fire carried out.

16. ACKNOWLEDGE.

Issued at 10 am 3/11/18.

Copy No. 1 to 172nd Inf. Bde.
" " 2 " DMGO 57th Div.
" " 3 " O.C. Sections
" " 4 " do.
" " 5 " do.
" " 6 " do.
" " 7 " O.C. 2/4 KAR
" " 8 " O.C. Barrage Group.
" " 9 } War Diary
" " 10 }
" " 11 Spare.
" " 12

[illegible]
Capt.
Comndg 172nd M.G. Coy.

War Diary

W9/30.

SECRET. Machine Gun Barrage for Raid by 2/4th K.O.R. COPY No 9

SECRET. Group Commander's Orders.

1. A runner from each Battery will be sent to M.G. Dugout HEADQUARTERS WALK I 10c 55.75. He will report there at ZERO – 1 hour.

2. Guns will be in position and ready to fire at ZERO – 30 mins. This will be reported to me by Battery commanders.

3. The following code will be used in connection with this raid :–

Operation cancelled	POTATO.	Few casualties	TOMATO.
Men formed up	CRESS.	Held up	LETTUCE.
Raid successful	MUSTARD.	Party all in	CARROT
All doing well	CELERY.	Artillery & Infys. to continue an extra 10 minutes viz Zero + 50 till Zero + 60.	CUCUMBER.
Much resistance	BEANS.		
Weak do	PEAS.		
Prisoners returning	SEEDS.	Operations postponed 60 minutes, to be sent 30 minutes before ZERO.	CABBAGE.
Many casualties	ONIONS.		

4. Rifle Grenades bursting into 2 REDS and 2 WHITES will be the signal for the Artillery and Machine Guns to keep on the Barrage an extra ten minutes. This signal will be sent up by O.C. Raid, repeated at HEADQUARTERS WALK and Battalion H.Qrs. Each battery will post a special lookout.

5. Battery Commanders at I 3 b 00.15, I 9 a 00.50, I 8 d 80.35 and I 14 d 18.70 will endeavour to establish lamp communication with each other. For this purpose 172nd M.G. Coy will lend 171st M.G. Coy two signalling lamps.

6. Guns will remain in position ready to put down a further barrage till Zero + 120 mins. after which usual dispositions will be taken up.

7. Group Commander will be at H.Q. of O.C. Operations at Coy. H.Q. HEADQUARTERS WALK, I 10c 70.85.

8. M.G. Coys will please ACKNOWLEDGE.

Copies to :–
No. 1–4 170, 171, 172 & 173 M.G. Coys.
No. 5. DMGO 57th Div.
No. 6. 172nd Inf. Bde.
No. 7. 2/4 K.O.R.
No. 8–10 Spare.

G. H. Wade Capt.
Commdg. M.G. Barrage Group
57th Div.

30/1/18.

No 2.

SECRET. Relief Order. Copy No 2.

1. By daylight on 2[illegible] February 1918 the 172nd M.G.Coy. will be relieved by 171st M.G.Coy. in the ARMENTIERES sector.
No 1 section will then relieve the Section of 171 M.G.Coy now in HOUPLINES under arrangements made by Section Officers concerned and will take up the following dispositions:- FARM POST, HERRING CORNER, DURHAM CASTLE and JAMES CORNER.
This Section will be attached to 173 M.G.Coy.

2. Belt boxes & tripods except those taken into the line on the 21st inst. which will be brought back to Coy H.Q. will be handed over to incoming unit who will leave an equivalent number at Coy. H.Qrs. on their way to the line.

3. Relieving Company will leave Coy H.Qrs at 11-30 a.m. & their limbers will bring back material of this Company.

4. All particulars with reference to work done, S.O.S. line, fields of fire etc will be handed over most fully.

5. Emplacements, dugouts & latrines will be left perfectly clean.
Certificates will be obtained by each Section Officer to this effect and handed in to C.O. at Coy H.Qrs. after relief. Also receipts in triplicate for all trench stores handed over.

6. The N.C.O. in charge of the Foot Washing Centre will obtain receipts for all stores handed over. No socks will be handed over but will be taken to TISSAGE DUMP and placed on limber returning to H.Q.

7. After relief sections will return to Coy H.Qrs & will there receive further instruction as to proceeding to billets in the STEENWERCK area.

8. No guides will be required for 171st M.G.Coy.

9. Transport Officer will arrange for limbers to be at Coy H.[illegible] to convey guns & material to STEENWERCK area at 3 p.m.

10. Mobile reserve will be left by 171st Coy at their present Transport Lines STEENWERCK & by 173rd Coy. at their Transport lines at PONT NIEPPE.
Transport Officer will be responsible that S.A.A. at STEENWERCK is checked on arrival there.

11. All details as to move of Q.M. Stores, Officers Messes etc will be arranged by 2 i/c.

12. One house in ARMENTIERES is permanently allotted for sole use of this Company and one for sole use of 171st M.G.Coy. All stores etc. not likely to be wanted at STEENWERCK during next seven days will be dumped there.

13. Ptes. Roberts, Saundle, Smeafitt & Jones (Joiner) will remain in the house and will be rationed by 171st M.G.Coy.

14. ACKNOWLEDGE.

Distribution

Copy No		Copy No	
1	172nd Inf Bde	9	O.C. 171st M.G.Coy.
2	War Diary	10	O.C. 172nd M.G.Coy.
3	Ditto	11	" 173rd M.G.Coy.
4	2 i/c	12	M.G. Oatershott
5	O.C. No 1 Section	13	Spare.
6	" 2 "	14	
7	" 3 "		
8	" 4 "		

[illegible] 2/Lt
for O.C. 172 M.G.Coy.
[illegible]/18

No 3

SECRET — Relief of 171 M. G. Coy. — Copy No 13

MAP REF: Sheet 36 N.W.

1. By daylight on the 5th Feby 8 guns of 172 M. G. Coy. will relieve 8 guns of 171 M. G. Coy. in and forward of the subsidiary line in the L'EPINETTE Section.
2. 4 guns of 172 M. G. Coy. will relieve 4 guns of 173 M. G. Coy. at BOULOGNE, FOLKESTONE, SIBERIA & HELENE M.G. emplacements in the Defences of ARMENTIERES.
3. These reliefs will be complete before 1-0 p.m.
4. Belt boxes & tripods may be exchanged under arrangements made by Section Officers.
5. No 1 Section of 172 M. G. Coy. now in HOPLINES will be relieved at 12 noon by 1 Section of 171 M.G. Coy. No 1 Section will then proceed to the LAUNDRIES H.[illegible] 5.8.
6. Guides found by 173 M. G. Coy. will be at [illegible] C.27.c.4.9. at 10-0 a.m. and details of the relief are as [illegible]
7. Mobile Reserve S.A.A. will be loaded in the [illegible] S.A.A. limbers.
8. The Company will parade in full marching [illegible] packs, at 7-0 a.m. in road outside orderly room ready to proceed to trenches via ERQUINGHEM Bridge, 200 [illegible] between Sections. Packs will be put on Section limbers, blankets rolled in bundles of 5 will be on limbers i.e. on scale of one per man. Limbers will be packed before 6-30 a.m. Surplus blankets in bundles of 10 will be at Q. M. Stores before 6-30 a.m.
   All palliasses will be handed in to Q.M. Stores before 6-30 a.m.
9. Transport Officer will arrange for limbers to be at Sections billets at 6-0 a.m.
10. Officers horses will parade at Orderly Room at 7-0 a.m.
11. All billets must be left perfectly clean & Section Officers will personally inspect their men's accommodation before time of parade.
    Latrines will be filled in at 6-30 a.m.
12. [illegible] taken over will be [illegible] to Coy. [illegible] as soon as possible.
13. [illegible] will be provided by 171 M. G. Coy.
14. Packs will be left at Coy H.Q. except those belonging to the Sections in Reserve.
15. Attention is drawn to attached system of fighting "Trench Feet"
16. ACKNOWLEDGE.

Distribution:

1. H.Q. 170th Inf Bde.
2. H.Q. 171st Inf. Bde.
3. 171st M. G. Coy.
4. 173rd M. G. Coy.
5. C.O.
6. O.C. No 1 Section
7. 2/Lt. [illegible]
8. O.C. No 2 Section.
9. O.C. No 3 Section.
10. O.C. No 4 Section.
11. Transport Officer
12. 2 i/c.
13. } War Diary.
14. }

[signature] 2/Lt
for O.C. 172 M. G. Coy.

4-2-18.

RELIEF TABLE.

SECTION	ACTION TO BE TAKEN	REMARKS.	CODE WORD TO REPORT Relief Complete
1.	Will be relieved by 4 guns of 171st M.G. Coy & proceed to LAUNDRIES H.5.a.6.8.	Relief commences 12 noon.	OPEN.
2.	Will relieve 4 guns of 171st M.G. Coy at RAILWAY, SALIENT, QUALITY & [illegible]	Relief to be completed before 1 p.m.	TOOT
3.	Will relieve 4 guns of 171st M.G. Coy at SQUARE Cts, HALT, LOTHIAN, CENTRAL	do	TREAT.
4.	Will relieve 4 guns of 171st M.G. Coy at BOULOGNE, [illegible], SIBERIA & HELENE	Section of 172 Coy will leave Section H.Q. [illegible] 10 a.m.	FOAL.

System of Fighting Trench Foot.

1. This will be exactly the same as that used in the last tour in the line.

2. The Foot Washing Centre will be at I.2.b.5.8. & all men proceeding to it will use LUNATIC LANE.

3. Sgt. Wood will be in charge & O.C. No 1 Section will instruct him to report to 2/Lt. G.C. Prince at H.Q. Section [illegible] C.24.c.4.9. at 10 am 5/2/18. The men detailed to assist him will be there at that time. 2 i/c will make arrangements for this & will arrange for supply of everything necessary. 2/Lt. [illegible] will choose a house suitable for Foot Washing Centre at above map ref.

4. Officer i/c guns in BOULOGNE – HELENE line will be responsible for the Foot Washing Centre & will frequently visit it.

5. Men will proceed for treatment daily from & including 6/2/18.

4-2-18.

[illegible] 2/Lt

for O.C. 172 M.G. Coy

No 4

SECRET

Ref Map. 36 NW 1/10,000.
HOUPLINES 9a
BOIS GRENIER 8a.

172nd Machine Gun Coy. Order No. 11.

Copy No. 7

1. Today at ZERO HOUR a party of 2/7 Btn. K.L.R will raid enemy Front Line from C 29 a 45.10 to C 29 a 60.50.
2. Raid will be supported by Artillery and M.G. Barrage.
3. Guns of this company will fire as detailed in attached table.
4. Should it be necessary to postpone the Operation the code word will be sent so as to reach Group H.Q. by Zero - 40 minutes.

Operations Postponed	SUN, followed by the number of minutes.		
do cancelled	MOON	Held up	SEA.
Have formed up.	STAR.	Party all in	STREAM.
Raid successful	SNOW.	Artillery to continue an extra ten mins	RAIN.
All doing well	FROST.		
Prisoners returning	THAW.		
Many casualties	WATER		
Few do.	RIVER		

5. ZERO hour will be eight thirty pm. tonight. 6/2/18.
6. In event of communication breaking down gun commanders will conform to action of artillery.
7. Right and Left divisions will be supplied by Artillery on Z night on the CELT System from Z-10 to Z-3 and on enemy's Front & Support Line in I 22 a & I 16 d from Z-10 to Z-3.
8. A runner from each officer having guns cooperating will be sent to M.G. Dugout C 22 c 60.00 (in Subsidiary Line right of GLOUCESTER AV) He will report there at Zero - 1 hour.
9. Guns will be ready to fire at Zero - 30 mins. & a report that they are ready will be sent to Group Commander. Guns will remain in position till Zero + 95 mins. after which usual dispositions will be taken up.

Group Commander, Lieut. Blackman will be at HQ. 2/7 K.L.R. (C 22 c 7.1)

ACKNOWLEDGE.

Copies to.

1 D.M.G.O.
2 Lt Blackman.
3 O.C. No. 1 Section
4 " " 3
5 " " 4 172nd M.G. Coy.
6 172nd Inf. Bde
7 War Diary
8 " "
9-12 Spare.

E. Aldridge
Capt.
Comndg 172nd M.G. Coy

Serial No.	Gun Position	Task, Standing Barrage on:–	GRID direction	Elevation	Time & Rate	Remarks.
1.	HELENE C 27c 50.60	Part of E.F.45. Lines from	72° – 75°	6°	Zero to Zero+5	
	SIBERIA. C 27c 14.34	C 29a 80.67 to	68° – 72°	8°43'	250 per min.	
	FOLKESTONE I 2b 91.91.	C 23c 83.73	63° – 68°	9°40'	Zero+5 to	
2.	I 9-2	C 29a 9.1	44°	7°51'	Zero+25	1° Traverse each way
–	I 3-2	C 29b 13.	53°	4°32'	100 per min.	do.
3.	BOULOGNE I 2b 69.65.	Enemy F.45 Line from.	79°-83°	9°11'		
	I 3-1.	C 29c 50.80. to C 29c 90.40.	48°-52°	4°48'		

No 5

SECRET [illegible]

[illegible]

1. On [illegible] the [illegible] M.G. Coy will be relieved by [illegible] the [illegible] SECTION.
2. O.C. Sections will arrange for a guide from each [illegible] to [illegible] of [illegible] [illegible] [illegible]
[illegible]
O.C. No 3 Section will [illegible] a guide to [illegible] will [illegible] at [illegible] for each [illegible]
3. Belt boxes will be handed over [illegible] other gun equipment will be brought out of the line.
The limbers of the relieving Company will [illegible] bring back all material belonging to the Company.
4. Maps, emplacement books, [illegible] books, [illegible] aeroplane photographs, orders relating to [illegible] defence, armour piercing S.A.A. [illegible] A.B. [illegible] forms will be handed over and receipts obtained.
5. All material at the [illegible] including the notice board will be brought back [illegible] arrangements to be made by O.C. No 3 Section.
Personnel at [illegible] will not be relieved but will proceed to Coy. H.Q. as soon as [illegible] in limber.
6. All dugouts, emplacements, latrines etc. belonging to this Company will be handed over scrupulously clean & a receipt on attached form obtained & handed to O.C. Company at Coy. H.Qrs. after relief.
7. It cannot be too strongly impressed upon all ranks how vitally important it is that every detail is handed over accurately to the relieving team.
8. After relief sections will proceed independently to Coy. H.Qrs.
9. Transport Officer will arrange for [illegible] limbers to be at [illegible] at 4 p.m.
10. All [illegible] Officers' valises etc. will be loaded on motor lorry at 10 a.m.
The cook taking sufficient number of [illegible] will travel with this lorry & on arrival in new area will [illegible] food & tea so that the Company can be fed immediately on arrival at billets.
One N.C.O. from each section & [illegible] who will be responsible for officers' baggage [illegible] by lorry.
Adjutant will be responsible for [illegible]
11. C.Q.M.S. will [illegible] [illegible] [illegible] [illegible] [illegible]
12. Orders for relief of No 1 Sect. will be issued by [illegible]
13. Adjutant will ensure that billets & [illegible] are [illegible] [illegible] certificate to that effect.
14. ACKNOWLEDGE.

Issued at 8.30 p.m.

[illegible]

[illegible]-18.

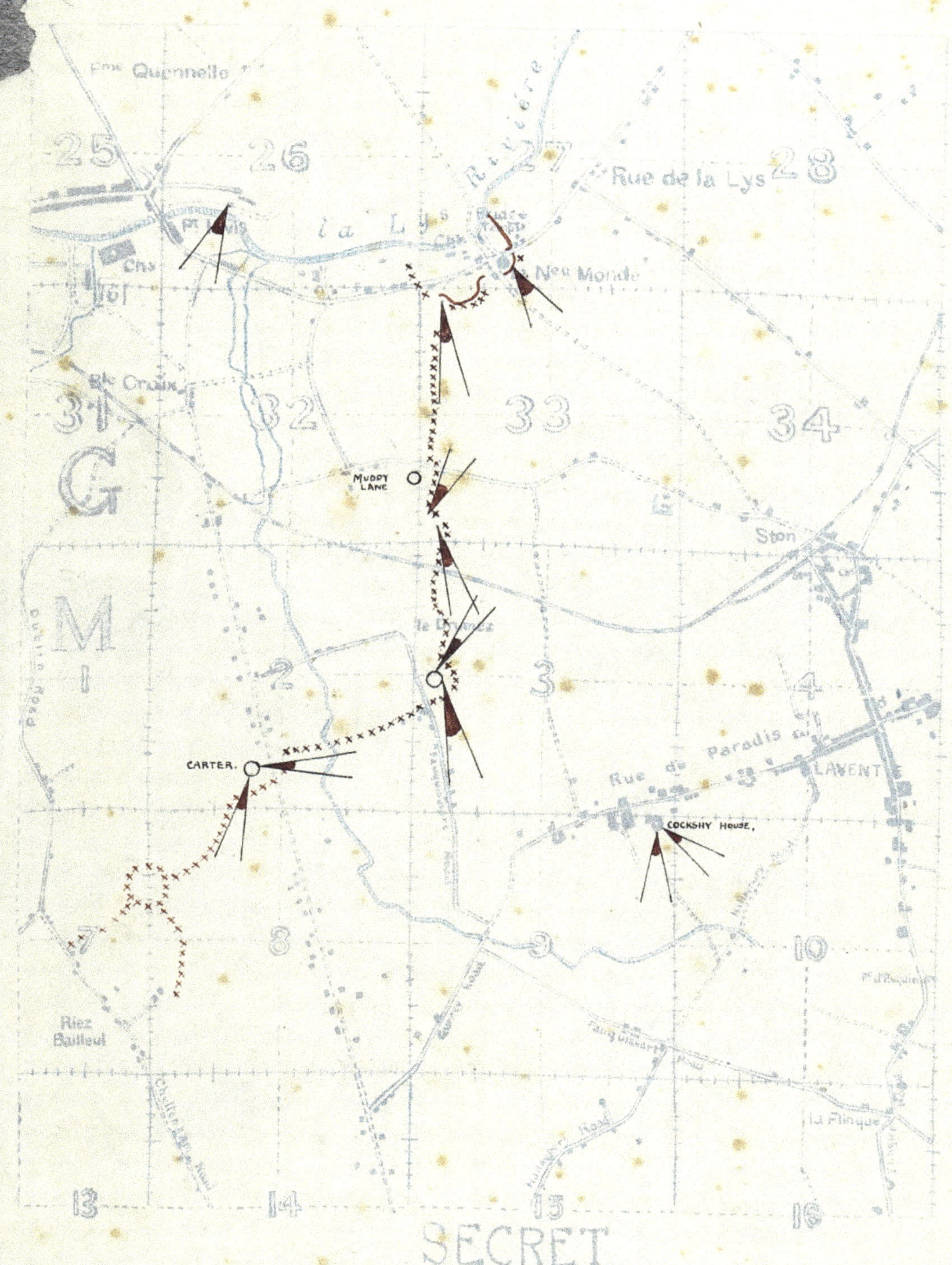

Scale 1: 20,000. 172nd MACHINE GUN COY

www.ingramcontent.com/pod-product-compliance
Lightning Source LLC
Chambersburg PA
CBHW081428160426
43193CB00013B/2224